The Beginner's Guide to Fasting

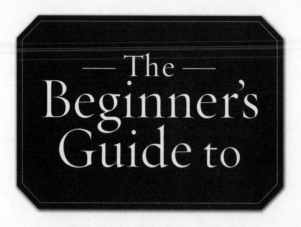

The Beginner's Guide to

Fasting

ELMER L. TOWNS

Regal

From Gospel Light
Ventura, California, U.S.A.

Published by Regal
From Gospel Light
Ventura, California, U.S.A.
www.regalbooks.com
Printed in the U.S.A.

Originally published by Servant Publications in 2001.
Second edition published by Regal in 2009.

Library of Congress Cataloging-in-Publication Data
Towns, Elmer L.
The beginner's guide to fasting / Elmer Towns.
p. cm.
Includes bibliographical references.
ISBN 978-0-8307-4604-0 (trade paper)
1. Fasting—Religious aspects—Christianity. I. Title.
BV5055.T685 2009
248.4'7—dc22
2008051804

2 3 4 5 6 7 8 9 10 11 12 13 14 15 / 15 14 13 12 11 10

Rights for publishing this book outside the U.S.A. or in non-English languages
are administered by Gospel Light Worldwide, an international not-for-profit ministry.
For additional information, please visit www.glww.org, email info@glww.org, or
write to Gospel Light Worldwide, 1957 Eastman Avenue, Ventura, CA 93003, U.S.A.

Contents

I was converted to Christ at age 17 and did not fast until I was 39 years old. During those years I read the Bible through each year—including the passages on fasting—but never once thought fasting was for me. I considered fasting to be "an Old Testament thing" and I didn't feel the least bit concerned about not fasting until I moved to Lynchburg, Virginia, and met Jerry Falwell.

Jerry Falwell led his church to fast and it became part of our preparations in founding Liberty University. (I am called a co-founder, but Falwell was the driving force that established the university.) In Lynchburg, I found myself paying two monthly house payments, one in Virginia and another back in greater Chicago, because I couldn't sell my previous home before moving. Two monthly payments put an enormous strain on the family budget.

I observed that when Jerry Falwell needed money for a new university building or a television project, he asked people to fast and pray with him. The money always came in.

So I asked my wife to fast and pray with me on the fifteenth day of the month, because that was the date the Chicago mortgage payment was due. We fasted and prayed that month but the house didn't sell. I forgot about fasting until the fifteenth day of the following month, but then again it didn't sell.

After fasting and praying the third month, the realtor phoned to say there was finally a nibble. In a down real estate market, only one person looked at my house but he returned several times to check out details. We finally closed the sale almost one year after we first fasted. At the closing, the buyer told me he began looking at my house on his wife's birthday, the day after Ruth and I had fasted the very first time. I learned two things from that experience: First, fasting takes prayer to a higher level of fulfillment, and second, don't quit too soon.

That experience taught us that fasting is an invaluable foundation to prayer. Of course, not everything we have fasted about has happened, but fasting has added a new dimension to our prayer lives. Since that time, we have learned that fasting is an invaluable way to get to know God.

I challenge you to read this simple book and then follow its suggestions (unless you have a medical reason not to fast). When you embark upon your first fast, you are beginning a spiritual journey that will change your life. Not only are you more likely to get your prayers answered, you will draw closer to God than ever before.

Many people have taught me much about fasting. I give them credit for all the wisdom they have given me. For all the weaknesses in this book, I take responsibility. May God teach us all to "hunger and thirst after righteousness" so that we might know Him better.

Elmer L. Towns
www.elmertowns.com

Chapter One

Getting Ready to Fast

God created the human body as a finely tuned physical engine of enormous power, but it requires fuel to keep operating. That fuel is called food. To make sure the body gets fuel, God has created within us an appetite for food, called hunger. As part of the balance of nature to keep life going, food satisfies our appetite and gives us strength.

So why would one choose to go without food?

Americans are programmed to eat three times a day. We constantly hear the message, "A good breakfast is the foundation of the day." Our mothers told us, "Eat so you'll be strong," right along with, "Come in out of the rain so you won't catch a cold." In school we were taught, "Eat three square meals a day" and "Exercise to be strong." Since our childhood, we have been taught to take care of our bodies.

So why should one go without eating?

Starvation is still a worldwide threat. In 1978, I went to Haiti as part of a massive feeding program when that nation endured a famine, compounded by poverty. The swollen bellies of hungry little children distressed me. Starving people stampeded our vehicles for food, trampling fallen children just to get a loaf of bread. With much of the world clamoring for food like this, why would one voluntarily go without eating?

The world calls not eating dieting, and usually does it to lose weight or for health reasons. But some go without eating for spiritual reasons. The Bible calls this fasting. Usually a fast is for a predetermined length of time to accomplish a spiritual purpose.

Consider an example from the Old Testament. Once a year the Jewish believers were required to fast: "In the seventh month, on the tenth day, you shall go without eating" (Lev. 16:29, *CEV*). This fast was kept on the Day of Atonement, and so it is called the Yom Kippur Fast (the phrase means Day of Atonement). Conversely, there were seven other days in the Jewish calendar where believers were commanded to eat a "feast" because God realized there was great spiritual benefit in fellowship when believers eat together. But once each year on the Day of Atonement, God required His people to fast. Everyone went without eating. Why everyone? Because God wanted everyone to remember the solemn experience of his or her salvation. On the Day of Atonement, the high priest took the blood of an animal into the Holy of Holies to offer it in substitution for the sins of everyone: "And he shall wash his body with water in a holy place, put on his garments, come out and offer his burnt offering and the burnt offering of the people, and make atonement for himself and for the people" (Lev. 16:24). Because the Day of Atonement dealt with the sins of the nation, everyone fasted to identify with the High Priest, who sacrificed a lamb for the forgiveness of their sin.

Today, Christians are not required to fast; today we are not under law, but under grace. We no longer have to sacrifice the blood of a lamb for forgiveness. Jesus is the

Lamb of God who died for all (see John 1:29). In the Old Testament, Jewish believers fasted to demonstrate their obedience to God. However, in the New Testament's dispensation of grace, things are different. We are not *required* to fast, but we are *allowed* to fast for certain reasons. Jesus said to His disciples, "When you fast . . ." (Matt. 6:16) because fasting is a discipline to build our character and faith.

When you can't get an answer to prayer, even though you have prayed continually, try fasting with your prayer. Fasting demonstrates your sincerity to God: "If you believe with all your heart . . ." (Acts 8:37). When you give up food—that which is enjoyable and necessary—you get God's attention.

Even then, Jesus told us not to show off our fast: "Moreover, when you fast, do not be like the hypocrites, with a sad countenance. For they disfigure their faces that they may appear to men to be fasting" (Matt. 6:16). Jesus went on to explain what our attitude ought to be when we fast: "But you, when you fast, anoint your head and wash your face, so that you do not appear to men to be fasting, but to your Father who is in the secret place" (vv. 17-18).

If you have never fasted, it is probably a scary thing to think about going without food for any length of time. People have a variety of concerns because we are programmed to eat three times a day. Many wonder if they will get hungry and if the hunger pains will hurt.

Fasting to God will not hurt any more than dieting to get thinner. If you can cut back in your eating just to lose weight, you can cut back on food, in a reasonable way, to seek God's presence and get an answer to your prayers. Just as a diabetic has to stop eating sweets and someone with high blood pressure has to stop eating foods high in salt to stay healthy, you can fast for spiritual reasons.

Other people have different questions, such as, "Can I hold out?" They don't want to get started on a journey they can't complete. What if you see a commercial on television that suggests that a candy bar will help you get through the afternoon? Yes, chocolates and sugar will give you an afternoon "zap," but snacks are not always necessary. The ability to stay on your fast is not dependent upon how hard you try to stay away from food, but by how positive is the attraction of knowing God and spending time with Him.

Before I was converted, I was very religious, attending church every week. But I cursed all the time. Over the years, I tried several "religious" things to quit cursing but each time I slipped and began cursing again. The harder I tried, the more addictive the habit became. When I received Christ as my Savior, I instantly quit cursing—without trying and without religious tricks. Jesus made the difference. I no longer had any desire to curse; as a matter of fact, I abandoned cursing altogether. It is the same way with fasting. If you try "tricks" to keep from eating, there's a good chance you'll fail. But when you realize you'll spend quality time with Jesus while you are fasting, He will help you keep your fast. Remember the Scripture: "I can do all things through Christ who strengthens me" (Phil. 4:13).

There's another question people have about fasting: "Will I harm myself?" Because we've become so conditioned to eating three meals a day, we think we will harm ourselves when we miss those three meals. We think our bodies are like our cars: If we don't put oil in the engine, it'll burn up. Some think they'll get sick if they fast. And when they think of a three-day fast, they are absolutely sure they will die. But statistics have demonstrated that fasting is actually good for us. During a fast we eliminate poisons and toxins from the body. Just as God created the Sabbath day—one day out of seven—for rest, so a fast one day out of seven would give our digestive tract an opportunity to rest and be cleansed of built-up toxins.

Still others are concerned about what their friends will think if they fast. "Will my friends think I'm weird when they learn I am fasting?" The answer is simple: You don't fast to impress your friends, and on most occasions, you don't even let them know. As we've already seen, Jesus said, "When you fast, anoint your head and wash your face, so that you do not appear to men to be fasting, but to your Father who is in the secret place; and your Father who sees in secret will reward you openly" (Matt. 6:17-18).

Jesus was reminding us not to make an outward show of our religious dedication to God. Rather, fasting is a private commitment between you and God. Sometimes you fast privately and don't tell anyone. At other times, you will enter a public fast, such as with your church or with another individual (e.g., Ezra fasted with four thousand people to solve a problem, and Esther asked all Jewish believers to fast for divine intervention. Christians are asked to join the National Day of Prayer and Fasting in May each year.).

So don't worry what others think when you don't eat with them. Haven't there been occasions when you've gone on a coffee break with friends but just drank water? Or times when you've ordered only coffee at lunch because you have already eaten? Or just a soda because your stomach was upset? Be focused on your fast and don't pay attention to what others think. Just go ahead with your fast to God and keep your actions private.

What Is Fasting?

Fasting is not the same thing as dieting. And fasting is not the same thing as eliminating food for health. Fasting is a non-required discipline (you don't have to do it) where you alter your diet (there are many kinds of fasts) for a spiritual reason (there are many reasons to fast) and accompany the experience with prayer.

Fasting is not required of Christians. You don't have to do it. As a matter of fact, some who have never fasted may be more spiritual than some who do fast. For example, there are some grandmothers who are extremely effective intercessors even though they have never once fasted. Why? Because they continually live so close to God there is no need to fast to get closer to Him.

Take the illustration of a man who goes to the gym to exercise to keep in shape physically. He can keep in shape by any means of daily exercise, whether he uses barbells, a rowing machine, a skiing machine, or simply jogs. Each form of exercise is a discipline that keeps him in good physical condition. But there is another man who keeps in great shape without ever going to the gym or jogging. He's a roofer who keeps in shape by constantly throwing around house shingles.

Like the grandmother or the roofer, you may already stay close to God and keep "spiritually fit" even without fasting. But fasting is a biblical discipline that will help anyone get into spiritual shape and become a prayer warrior for God.

When you fast, expect resistance. Our spiritual enemy, the devil, will oppose you. As you may have already experienced when you have repented or transformed certain areas of your life, the devil does not easily give up any territory he has conquered. So it is with prayer and fasting. If you pray for others—for your church or for the salvation of people—Satan will oppose you. Fasting is not easy. Like climbing a mountain, fasting is spiritually as well as physically challenging. It can be difficult, draining and dangerous. So embark on this adventure with full understanding of what you are doing and full knowledge that the path ahead may be tough. But the rewards will be worth it.

Principles I Learned About Getting Ready

· The one-day Yom Kippur Fast is best for my first fast.

· I should not be fearful about fasting, because many have gone without food for one day.

· I am not required to fast, but I will do so as a spiritual discipline.

· I will not worry what others think about my fast because it is a personal commitment between God and me.

· I will expect spiritual resistance to my fast because the evil one does not want me to get closer to God.

Journaling

As you ponder a decision about whether or not you should fast, write your thoughts in your journal. The following questions will help to guide your decision-making process. Expressing yourself in writing will help you think more clearly and provide a record of your fasting journey.

1. Do you have a clear reason to fast? What is it? (This is usually called a cause.)

2. List some reasons why you should not fast, or any times when you shouldn't fast.

3. Make a list of the difficulties you think you'll encounter in your fast. Why are they problems to you?

4. Do you think you can overcome them? How?

Three-Step Bible Study

The Bible studies at the end of each chapter are designed to lead you in the study of God's Word in three easy steps.

· First, read the question and focus on how the topic applies to your life.

· Second, read and analyze the related Bible verse that is given for that question. Think about what the Scripture is saying to you.

· Third, write your response to the question. Even when you think the answer is simple, writing it out makes you think more exactly and will provide a helpful record for you later.

1. God required all Israelites to fast, but this is not a requirement for the present-day church. What lessons can Israel's fasting have for you?

   "On the tenth day of the seventh month of each year, you must go without eating" (Lev. 16:29, CEV).

   _____

   _____

   _____

   _____

   _____

   _____

2. What can you learn from Jesus about fasting? How will this verse influence your fasting?

   "But you, when you fast, anoint your head, and wash your face, so that you do not appear to men to be fasting, but to your Father who is in the secret place; and your Father who sees in secret will reward you openly" (Matt. 6:17-18).

   _____

   _____

   _____

   _____

   _____

3. You must fast with outward repentance as well as with inward sincerity. How have you prepared (or will you prepare) for your first fast?

" 'Now, therefore,' says the Lord, 'Turn to Me with all your heart, With fasting, with weeping, and with mourning' " (Joel 2:12).

_____

_____

_____

_____

_____

_____

_____

_____

4. What will God do for you when you fast?

"So rend your heart, and not your garments; Return to the Lord your God, for He is gracious and merciful, Slow to anger, and of great kindness; And He relents from doing harm. Who knows if He will turn and relent, and leave a blessing behind Him" (Joel 2:13-14).

_____

_____

_____

_____

_____

_____

_____

_____

5. What should be the prayer of your heart about unknown sin as you begin a fast?

"Search me, O God, and know my heart; Try me, and know my anxieties; And see if there is any wicked way in me, and lead me in the way everlasting" (Ps. 139:23-24).

_____

_____

_____

_____

_____

_____

_____

6. What will it take to seek and find God? What do you have to do to find Him?

"And you will seek Me, and find Me, when you search for Me with all your heart" (Jer. 29:13).

_____

_____

_____

_____

_____

_____

_____

_____

Chapter Two

My First Fast

In the preface I told you about my first fast when my wife and I were praying to sell a second house we owned. But you may not be able to identify with my first fasting experience. Because I am a full-time minister, you may think, *Well, you're supposed to do things like that.* Then let me tell you about my granddaughter's first experience with fasting.

Beth is in the sixth grade and works on the puppet team in the Sunday night youth group at our church. The group planned to go to our city's juvenile detention center to entertain and present the gospel through a puppet presentation. On her own, Beth decided to do a one-day fast, praying that some in the audience might pray to receive Christ. This was scary for Beth, because she had never done anything like this before and she was doing it alone. (The team did not fast.)

She planned a one-day Yom Kippur Fast, from sundown to sundown. (This fast is explained in more detail later in this chapter.) On the afternoon before her fast, she ate a snack when she got home from school, and then began her fast at sundown. She went without the evening meal, spending some time in her room praying for the puppet presentation. The next day she didn't eat breakfast or lunch. During lunch she prayed at her desk.

"It was hard," she told me. "All I could think about all day was eating." Then her twelve-year-old innocence confessed, "I was glad the sun went down early (in late fall) so that I could eat a snack before dinner."

While it may appear to be a simple thing, it was a huge step of faith for her. And what was the result of Beth's fast? Several in the juvenile home prayed to receive Christ because those of the same age presented the gospel to them. In the same way, God will honor your first step of faith, which may seem a small step to others, but be a giant one for you.

As for Beth, a one-day fast may be a good place to begin if you have never fasted before. Remember, God is more concerned about the response of your heart than He is in the length of the fast. Jesus observed that some thought their prayers were heard and answered "for their many words" (Matt. 6:7). However, God responds to your prayer not according to how long you pray, but how sincerely you pray. The same is true for fasting.

When a man proposes to a woman, it is not the length of his proposal that gets a "YES!"; it is his heart that counts. And so when you begin fasting, don't be concerned with how long your fast should last. Just make sure your relationship with God is healthy.

God knows all things. He understands and regards the sincerity of your prayers over and above the length of your prayers. Jesus said, "For your Father knows the things you have need of before you ask Him" (Matt. 6:8).

So, if you have never fasted, begin with a one-day Yom Kippur Fast. As mentioned in chapter one, in the Old Testament the Jews were required to fast for one day each year on Yom Kippur. According to the Jewish timetable, a day began at sundown and ended the following day at sundown. The Jews learned to count their days from God, "So the evening and the morning were the first day" (Gen. 1:5).

Plan to start your fast when the sun goes down, or perhaps a little before the sun goes down. This means you are going to do without the normal evening meal, then skip breakfast and lunch the following day. Most Jews ended their fast by eating a normal meal after the sun went down.

When the pastor of my local church calls our congregation to prayer, we usually begin a church-wide fast late Sunday afternoon. Sunday morning my pastor announces, "Eat a small snack before you come to church on Sunday evening. We will begin fasting together during the Sunday evening service. If you go out for a Sunday evening snack with other believers after church, don't eat any solid food; just have coffee. Don't break your fast until the sun goes down on Monday evening when you eat your normal evening meal."

Why does my pastor tell our congregation to eat a small snack before we begin? There were occasions in the Old Testament when God told His people to prepare for a fast by eating before they began. He told Elijah, "Arise and eat, because the journey is too great for you" (1 Kings 19:7). What was the result? "So he arose, and ate and drank; and he went in the strength of that food forty days and forty nights as far as Horeb, the mountain of God" (v. 8).

Fast with a Friend

Even though this book is focused on private prayer and fasting—which is the foundation of all intercession—perhaps, if you have never walked this road before, you should begin your fasting journey with another person. If you are fasting for a specific answer to prayer, ask someone else to pray and fast with you; there is strength in corporate prayer. Jesus said, "If two of you agree on earth concerning anything that they ask, it will be done for them by My Father in heaven" (Matt. 18:19). This verse does not speak only about prayer; it is a reference to the commitment we make in agreement with someone else.

Think about it this way. When you plan to go on a vacation with someone else, it is more memorable if you plan together, dream together, and share experiences together. You probably get more out of a vacation when you share your experience with someone else. The same with fasting: When you share the experience of fasting and praying together, you probably have more focus in your prayers.

But fasting with another also provides other benefits. You have someone you can talk with about doubts, or questions, or fears. If fasting is scary to you, the strength of another person can help you get through the experience. You can always phone each other for support and ask, "How's it going?" That phone call may give you the courage to keep going.

And don't forget the celebration. When you climb the mountain alone, you climb to prove something to yourself and the victory belongs to you only. But when you climb the mountain with others, you have many to rejoice with when the victory is won. You cheer, hug, and then come back down to tell everyone about the victory. When you finish fasting together, you can rejoice together. Mere *togetherness* makes victory sweeter.

Another positive aspect of fasting with a friend is that it creates accountability. When you know that a friend is aware of your fast, you will not be tempted to sneak a snack or violate your fast. Maybe you've jogged or walked for better health with a friend before. If so, you know how having a partner helps you stay committed when the going gets hard. If you're strong, you won't need someone to help you with accountability, but if not, then partnering with someone who's in the same boat may help.

Fast with a Purpose

When you get ready to fast, go deep within your heart to determine the reason you are fasting. There are many reasons to fast and in later chapters we will examine them. You may already have a reason to fast; otherwise, you wouldn't be reading this book.

"Is there not a cause?" (1 Sam. 17:29), young David said when he went out to face Goliath. No other soldier from Israel would face the giant. Not only would they not fight Goliath, each gave David a different reason to discourage him from the battle. But David would not be deterred; he had deep cause to fight this particular giant and this battle. David was willing to die fighting the enemy of God.

It isn't just a matter of praying and giving up food. We must fast for a reason. Are you willing to die to appetite and pleasure by fasting? When you relinquish your desires for a higher purpose, you are assuming the same attitude as David when he asked, "Is there not a cause?"

Write down your cause. Put it into writing so that you can see it with your own eyes. Sometimes when you keep a cause wrapped up in your mind, it remains blurred or vague. Right now, you may have a generalized feeling about why you should be fasting, but take the time to get your cause on paper. When you see it written down, it will sharpen your focus. Fill out the Fasting Purpose Sheet below. Note the place to write out the purpose of your fast. Doing this will help you clarify your reason for fasting and record your cause for future reference.

Fasting Purpose Sheet

My cause or reason for fasting:

_____

Who I will ask to fast with me (if anyone):

_____

I will fast:

Begin date: _____   Time: _____

End date: _____   Time: _____

I believe that God is the only answer to my request and that prayer without fasting is not enough to get an answer to my need. Therefore, by faith I am fasting because I need God to work in this matter.
God being my strength and grace being my basis, I commit myself to the above fast.

_____

Signed/Date

Plan Everything

Don't enter your fast casually or with a "hit or miss" attitude. Plan to succeed; if you don't, you probably won't.
Don't enter your fast just to see how far you can go. Some
people have fasted with the attitude, "I'll try it until I get
hungry." Then at the first sign of discomfort, they give
up. Make a commitment to fast for one day, no matter
what. The Purpose Sheet has a place for you to indicate
when you will begin and end (time and date) your fast.

Filling out your Purpose Sheet does not guarantee
you will fast successfully, but thinking through your purpose ahead of time will help you be more resolute during
your fast. When you sign your Purpose Sheet, you have
moved from just thinking about fasting and wishing to
be more spiritual; you have stepped up to a higher level
and made a commitment to seek God for your cause.

Just as there are many factors that usually influence
any significant decision, a decision to fast occurs in several phases or layers, just as there are layers on lettuce or
cabbage. First, we begin with a *wish*, or something that we
dream of doing but think will never happen. We dream
of touching God with our prayers, and then letting God
touch us.

Second, we move from a wish to a deep driving *desire*.
In the first step, we *want* to touch God; in the second, we
must touch God. Our wish becomes passion. The deeper
we think about our decision to touch God, the more our
decision becomes a part of our psyche or personality. We
are saying, "I must touch God; I won't be spiritually whole
until I touch God." The third step involves *planning*. Our

burning desire forces us to think and plan ways to accomplish our dream.

The fourth step is *imprinting*, where the decision becomes us and we become our goal. Our whole person is committed to carry out our decision and plan to touch God and be touched by Him.

Deciding to fast produces a two-way power. Like a long freight train where one engine pulls and another engine pushes, when you make a life-changing decision to fast, two powers kick in. You have the human power of your decision, but you also have the divine power of God. The Lord will help you fast, probably at the level of your commitment to fast.

A Commitment of Grace

Even though your Purpose Sheet has a place for you to sign your commitment, this is not a legalistic pledge. Rather, it is a pledge that depends on God's mercy. Note the phrase, "God being my strength, and grace being my basis." You're not saying, "I hope to fast," nor are you saying, "I want to fast." You are committing yourself to fast based on grace and God's help. You are *not* making a bargain with God that if you go without food for a day, you expect Him to answer your prayers. That's legalism. The basis of your fast is grace. Just as you can do nothing to wash away your sins (only God does that), so you do not have any power in yourself to answer your prayer. You depend on God's power. Grace says God does it all. You yield yourself to Him and wait for His power to answer your prayer.

Principles I Learned About My First Fast

· I must begin fasting in a simple way for a single purpose.

· I will be accountable if I fast with a friend.

· I will fast more successfully if I carefully consider my purpose and write it down.

· I must make a commitment up front when to begin and end a fast, not try to see how long I can hold out.

Journaling

Even before beginning your fast, write the thoughts you have as you consider your decision to fast. Describe your wish and your desire for what your fasting will accomplish. The following questions will guide you to fulfilling your purpose.

1. Write out the fears you have about fasting. Sometimes you diminish your fears when you get your fears out of your heart and put them on paper.

2. Write out the cause that is motivating you to fast. (Use the Fasting Purpose Sheet.)

3. Make a list of the people who might join you in this fast. Then give the reasons why you might choose one to join you.

4. Besides the cause for which you fast, what do you think this fast will do for you spiritually?

5. Notice that the Purpose Sheet reminds you that fasting is based on grace. Some think that fasting is a legalistic tool, i.e., "If I deprive myself of food, God will answer my prayers." Write why you think this fast is not legalistic.

Three-Step Bible Study

- Read the question.
- Read and analyze the Bible verse.
- Write out your response to the question.

1. Since the average Old Testament believers demonstrated their faith with a one-day Yom Kippur Fast, what can you learn from their example?

   "On the tenth day of the seventh month of each year, you must go without eating to show sorrow for your sins, and no one, including foreigners who live among you, is allowed to work" (Lev. 16:29, CEV).

   _____

   _____

   _____

   _____

   _____

   _____

   _____

2. One of the most important aspects of fasting is having a cause or purpose. What is the cause of your prayer-fast? What has God promised?

   "And whatever you ask in My name, that I will do, that the Father may be glorified in the Son. If you ask anything in My name, I will do it" (John 14:13-14).

   _____

   _____

   _____

   _____

   _____

3. What are some wrong reasons for prayer and fasting? One wrong reason is found in this verse. Are these reasons why you are fasting?

   "And when you pray, do not use vain repetitions as the heathen do. For they think that they will be heard for their many words" (Matt. 6:7).

   _____

   _____

   _____

   _____

   _____

4. Many begin their first fast with a friend. Give the name of a friend you'd like to join you in a fast. What are some things you might do together?

"Again I say to you that if two of you agree on earth concerning anything that they ask, it will be done for them by My Father in heaven" (Matt. 18:19).

_____
_____
_____
_____
_____
_____
_____
_____

5. Jesus assumed His followers would fast. What should be your attitude when you fast?

"Moreover, when you fast, do not be like the hypocrites, with a sad countenance. For they disfigure their faces that they may appear to men to be fasting. Assuredly, I say to you, they have their reward. But you, when you fast, anoint your head and wash your face, so that you do not appear to men to be fasting, but to your Father who is in the secret place; and your Father who sees in secret will reward you openly" (Matt. 6:16-18).

_____
_____
_____
_____
_____
_____
_____
_____

6. Some are fearful to fast because they have never done it. But God tells you to do all things confidently. How can you overcome any fears about fasting?

"And whatever you do, do it heartily, as to the Lord and not to men, knowing that from the Lord you will receive the reward of the inheritance; for you serve the Lord Christ" (Col. 3:23-24).

_____

_____

_____

_____

_____

_____

_____

_____

_____

Chapter Three

What Kind of Fast?

Ron Phillips, pastor of Central Baptist Church, Hixson, Tennessee, called his congregation to a 40-day fast. The church had grown large so quickly that the building couldn't hold the people. What was the *purpose* of their 40-day fast? The congregation needed to build a new sanctuary and they had to decide how *large* to build it, *where* to build it, and *what kind* of building to construct.

Most of the pastoral staff entered a "normal" fast, that is, eating no solid food but only drinking juice for the 40-day period. But the pastor didn't ask the members to do a normal 40-day fast. Instead, he asked that each person commit to fast at his or her individual level of ability and availability during the 40 days. Some didn't eat desserts or meats; others fasted from two meals a day or fasted every other day. Some gave up other things, such as watching television, reading the newspaper, involvement in sports (golf, bowling, and so on), and other acceptable pursuits that were not evil in nature. Each committed himself or herself to some form of fasting. The purpose of the fast was not just to give up things, but for the congregation to use this time to pray and seek God's purpose for the future of the church. The pastor felt if all were seeking God's will, the congregation would come to a place of unity when it finally voted on the future of the church.

In this instance, the pastor put forth the purpose and length of the fast, but the church members individually chose the way they would fast. There are several ways you can fast, just as there are several ways you can pray. Conider some of the ways we pray. These can guide our fasting as well.

Thanksgiving . . . to give appreciation to God.
Praise . . . to exalt God.
Intercession . . . for the salvation of others.
Petition . . . asking for things.
Dedication . . . yielding to God.
Confessing . . . asking for forgiveness.
Communion . . . enjoying intimacy.
Worship . . . to magnify God.

Choose a way of fasting that compliments the *cause* or purpose for which you are seeking God's touch. When you are fasting you will want to talk to God in the way that best expresses your heart.

Six Types of Fasts

Before you begin your first fast, study the various ways people fasted in Scripture. Having knowledge will guide you to a better experience. (See *Fasting for Spiritual Breakthrough* by Elmer Towns, Regal Books, 1996, for a study of the various ways people of the Bible fasted.) The following list gives an overview of the types of fasts available to you. After you have surveyed the list, read the paragraph that explains each fast. The final section of this chapter will help you choose the fast that is appropriate for you.

- *Absolute Fast.* You eliminate both solid food and liquids. This is the most severe fast, used only for the most serious causes.

- *Normal Fast.* You eliminate solid food but drink liquids. Used by most believers when fasting.

- *Partial Fast.* You eliminate selected items from the diet, or selected meals.

- *John Wesley Fast.* You take only whole-grain bread and water for ten days in preparation for Christian service.

- *Rotation Fast (Mayo Clinic Fast).* You eat only one of the six food groups each day for six days for medical purposes.

- *Supernatural Fast.* A miracle in which Moses took neither food nor drink. Not recommended.

The Absolute Fast
This is a fast where you eliminate all food and water. Paul followed this type of fast for three days after he saw the Lord Jesus on the road to Damascus and was struck blind. "And he [Paul] was three days without sight, and neither ate nor drank" (Acts 9:9).

Do not follow the Absolute Fast in your first fast. This fast is designed for those who are deeply distressed or for those who are fasting to solve an extreme problem, such as deliverance from an addiction or protection from a spiritual enemy.

Also, this fast produces extreme physical consequences. God has made the body so that it cannot exist seven days without water. Going without water for a long time harms the membranes in the brain, producing permanent damage. You will probably die if you go longer than seven days without water, and any absolute fast for this period will produce serious results. Do not attempt an absolute fast for more than three days.

The Normal Fast

In this fast you eliminate all solid foods, drinking only liquids. In the Bible, fasting most often refers to people not eating solid food; the issue of drinking liquids is usually omitted. This is the way Luke described the 40-day fast of Jesus: "In those days He [Jesus] ate nothing, and afterward, when they had ended, He was hungry" (Luke 4:2). Notice nothing is said about Jesus drinking liquids.

What do people drink when they fast? I have interviewed and asked many people about this. Many Koreans fast while praying and most of them drink only water. Some drink only distilled or bottled water, not wanting to introduce chlorine or other chemicals into their bodies while fasting.

My pastor drank only black coffee during a 40-day fast, plus a Centrum vitamin pill each day. He felt fruit juice was merely a different composition of solid food, so his rule was to "drink nothing nutritious."

Others make a natural fruit drink by blending fresh fruit with a blender or mixer to stay with the natural element of the fast. Others drink vegetable juice or tomato juice from a can or bottle. Still others drink fruit juice, that is, orange, raspberry, grape, apple, or other flavor. Their argument is that in the Bible juice is not prohibited, and grape juice or milk may likely have been taken during a fast.

Some drink only a diet supplement, such as Boost or Ensure. A close friend fixed a milkshake each day with Slim-Fast and skim milk. That was his only daily intake.

When I fast, I eliminate enjoyable drink items such as soda and various forms of fruit drinks. I think this reflects the Old Testament description that they "afflicted themselves and fasted" (Isa. 58:3). My rule is "drink non-enjoyable liquids."

Remember, you fast to please God and not to please others or yourself. Ask God to lead you in what to drink, and fast with a good conscience toward God. Make sure you are comfortable with your fast in the presence of God, and eliminate anything that convicts your conscience: "But he who doubts is condemned if he eats, because he does not eat from faith" (Rom. 14:23). Drink only the liquid that glorifies God: "Whether you eat or drink, or whatever you do, do all to the glory of God" (1 Cor. 10:31).

The Partial Fast

In this fast you eliminate certain liquids or certain solids, but not all liquids and solids. This is also called the Daniel Fast because he would not eat at the king's table, but insisted, "Please test your servants for ten days, and let them give us vegetables to eat and water to drink" (Dan. 1:12). This fast did not hurt Daniel or his friends. At another time

Daniel reflected the spirit of the partial fast. "I ate no pleasant food, no meat or wine came into my mouth" (Dan. 10:3). This is a partial fast that specifically identifies what Daniel avoided: (1) *pleasant food*, which is similar to our doughnuts or cakes (a dessert fast); (2) *meat* (this was a non-meat diet); and (3) *wine*, that which is pleasurable or gives joy.

The John Wesley Fast

As the founder and leader of the great Methodist movement, Wesley brought all his parish preachers back to New Chapel, or London, for a conference every two or three months. To get ready spiritually for the conference, Wesley ate only bread (natural whole grain) and drank water for ten days prior to each conference. Wesley fasted and prayed for spiritual power to influence his ministries in these conferences. All agree that those Methodist preachers left the conference to change the world. Those preachers built the largest Protestant denomination in the world, a reflection that God honored Wesley's spiritual dedication of fasting and prayers.

The Rotation Fast (the Mayo Clinic Fast)

This fast has little use in Christian circles because it is used for medical purposes, primarily to discover a person's reaction or allergy to certain food groups. Usually, the patient has a one-day normal or absolute fast to cleanse his system. Then only one new food group is introduced (eaten) each day for six days, rotating through each of the six food groups. This helps to determine by elimination and exclusion what food is the source of a person's physical problem.

Supernatural Fast

This is a fast of no water or food that lasts for 40 days. Since the body usually can't live without water for more than seven days, this is a miraculous thing, and it can't be recommended for anyone today. This is what Moses did when he went to the top of Mount Sinai to receive the Ten Commandments.

How to Choose a Fast

There are several factors to consider when preparing to fast. Before deciding the best approach for you, take into account your specific situation. Here are some suggestions.

The First-Fast Factor

As mentioned in chapter 2, if you are facing your first fast, I suggest that you begin with the one-day Yom Kippur Fast. If you want to undertake a longer fast for a severe or ongoing problem, perhaps fasting one day a week for three weeks is better than beginning with a three-day fast. Remember, if this is your first fast, you are taking an uncharted journey. You will want to experiment cautiously because you are learning new skills and attitudes for both your body and soul.

Your first fast should be a Normal Fast, eating nothing, but drinking liquids for one day. This practice will help train your body so that it will not react negatively if you later eliminate both food and liquid.

The Matching Factor

You will want to match the *cause* of your fast with the type of fast. For a normal request, choose a Normal Fast. For a more severe problem, choose a fast that is more severe in its demands.

The Comfort Factor

You should be comfortable with both the length and the type of fast. Obviously, I don't mean physical comfort because fasting is described in the Bible as "afflicting yourself." But as you decide what you will eliminate when you pray, you should not "second guess" yourself, nor should you feel guilty that you are doing the wrong thing or something weird. Choose a type of fast that allows you to be comfortable with your decision.

The Time Factor

Obviously, many factors influence your choosing a fast or the length of a fast. You must consider your weekly schedule. What days of the week are impossible to fast? What special event is coming up when it is inadvisable to fast (Thanksgiving, Christmas, weddings, and the like)?

Never begin with a long fast. You don't know what to expect of your body, nor do you know how you will react emotionally. I find a one-day fast very easy. The same with a seven-day fast or 21-day fast. My 40-day fast was entirely enjoyable too. What I personally have the most difficulty with is a three-day fast. It has something to do with the expectations and the interactions between my body and my mind. Each person has unique experiences, so proceed slowly until you understand how you will react to a fast.

Whatever fast you choose as your first, remember that it is a step of faith. God will see your heart and reward you accordingly.

The Fasting Purpose Sheet in chapter two helped you focus on the cause or reason for your fast. The Fasting Planning Sheet that follows will help you think through factors that may affect your fast and help you determine the type of fast you will choose.

Fasting Planning Sheet

1. What is my purpose in fasting?

   _____

2. What is my biblical basis?

   _____

3. What are other factors that influence this fast?

   _____

4. What fast will I choose?

   _____

5. When will I fast? For how many days?

   _____

6. Why is this fast best at this time?

   _____

God being my strength, and grace being my basis, I commit myself to the above fast.

_____

Signed/Date

Don't Make Unnecessary Rules

I was addressing a group of eighty pastors in a southern city when I told them my pastor drank only black coffee when fasting. One pastor yelled from the rear of the room, "You can't do that!" Undaunted, I repeated the statement that my pastor had only black coffee during his 40-day fast. Again he yelled, "You can't do that!"

I smiled, and then said, "You're wrong." I pointed out the mistake in his English grammar: "You meant to say that he *shouldn't have* drunk coffee, which describes the correct method of drinking. But you said *you can't*, which described his *ability* to drink coffee. He did it . . ."

Then I told my interrupter to apply the "law of silence" when interpreting Scripture: *When God hasn't spoken, don't make rules.* God hasn't told us what to drink when fasting; He simply describes the fact that some drink when fasting. Similarly, God hasn't told us what *not* to drink. God is silent on these issues. Therefore, we shouldn't make rules about what to drink or not to drink when fasting.

Questions and misconceptions about fasting are many. There is no one set pattern for fasting. Many variables affect the type and length of fast we choose. We can't apply the same rules to all our fasting experiences. We must take into account our situation, our purpose, our spiritual condition, and our level of need. Since these will always be changing, so will the types of fasts we choose. Part of our growth is to learn what type of fast to apply to a particular problem.

Principles I Have Learned About Fasting

- I can fast in more than one way to effectively get answers to prayer.

- I should begin with a one-day Normal Fast.

- I should use the most severe type of fasting when I am facing the most severe problems.

- I will have my prayers answered by the sincerity of my heart, not by how much food and drink I withhold.

- I should not make rules about fasting where God has not spoken.

- I should ask God to lead me to the type of fast best for me, because there is no one set pattern to do it.

Journaling

As you plan a fast, take some time to record your thinking process regarding the type of fast you will use. Use the following questions to guide your decision making. Then write your answers in your journal.

1. List the reasons why you plan to fast. After you analyze the reasons, put them in the order of importance.

2. What do you want to accomplish with this fast, that is, what is your cause?

3. What do you think you will experience while fasting?

4. How did you arrive at the length of your fast?

5. How will the fast you are considering help you accomplish your cause?

6. What ideas or experiences is God using to lead you to a certain fast?

Three-Step Bible Study

· Read the question.
· Read and analyze the Bible verse.
· Write out your response to the question.

1. How serious was Paul's physical and spiritual condition that motivated him to take an Absolute Fast for three days? (Read Acts 9:1-9 and make a list of the issues facing Paul.)

   "And he was three days without sight, and neither ate nor drank" (Acts 9:9).

   _____

   _____

   _____

   _____

   _____

   _____

   _____

2. What characterized Jesus' 40-day fast? What can you learn from this fast?

"[Jesus was] tempted for forty days by the devil. And in those days He ate nothing, and afterward, when they had ended, He was hungry" (Luke 4:2).

_____

_____

_____

_____

_____

_____

_____

3. The leaders of the early church fasted. What can you learn from them?

"As they ministered to the Lord, and fasted, the Holy Spirit said, 'Now separate to Me Barnabas and Saul for the work to which I have called them.' Then, having fasted and prayed, and laid hands on them, they sent them away" (Acts 13:2-3).

_____

_____

_____

_____

_____

_____

_____

4. Obviously, you must be concerned about pleasing God when fasting. What should guide you?

"[Is] this not the fast that I have chosen: To loose the bonds of wickedness, To undo the heavy burdens, To let the oppressed go free, And that you break every yoke? Then your light shall break forth like the morning, Your healing shall spring forth speedily, And your righteousness shall go before you; The glory of the Lord shall be your rear guard" (Isa. 58:6,8).

_____

_____

_____

_____

_____

5. What should be your attitude toward fasting when other people try to tell you what to do or not do? Write what principles will guide your fast.

Remember the "law of silence": When God hasn't spoken, don't make rules.

_____

_____

_____

_____

_____

_____

_____

Chapter Four

Learning to Pray While Fasting

Have you ever tried to serve God and failed? Have you ever asked God to do something but He didn't answer your prayers? Think how the disciples felt when they tried something big and failed.

Jesus took three disciples—Peter, James and John—up to the top of the Mount of Transfiguration. He left nine disciples at the bottom of the mountain. A father brought his son to the nine so that they could cast a demon out of the boy, for the boy couldn't speak or hear. The disciples tried, but they couldn't cast out the demon. Can you imagine how embarrassing that must have been? They were surrounded by a supportive crowd that was looking for Jesus. The crowd was disappointed, the father was disappointed, the disciples were disappointed. The Pharisees and Temple spies were present, laughing in skepticism. No one was able to help the son.

But when the Lord came down the mountain, the father said to Jesus, "Lord, have mercy on my son, for he is an epileptic and suffers severely; for he often falls into the fire and often into the water" (Matt. 17:15). Jesus cast out the demon and Scripture tells us, "The child was cured from that very hour" (v. 18).

The nine disciples asked, "Why could we not do it?"

Jesus told them, "Because of your unbelief" (v. 20). It was their lack of faith. But at that time, the disciples did not ask how they could get more faith. They had only asked why they couldn't cast out the demon.

Jesus answered all their questions in one simple statement: "This kind does not go out except by prayer and fasting" (Matt. 17:21). In a simple formula, Jesus told them that prayer and fasting got answers; that prayer and fasting could heal the boy.

Maybe you're fasting because you've been praying but didn't get an answer. Maybe you need more faith. Jesus told them, "You will say to this mountain, 'Move from here to there,' and it will move; and nothing will be impossible for you" (Matt. 17:20). Whatever your motive, fasting will take prayer, coupled with faith, to a higher level. It will take you nearer to God.

Just because you fast, it doesn't mean God will automatically hear or answer your prayers. Also, refraining from food will not make you more spiritual. Spirituality is a response of the heart to God when you seek His presence and yield to Him. The Holy Spirit will make you more holy when you allow the Lord to flow through your life. The Holy Spirit will make you more spiritual when you are filled with His presence. Remember, as you fast, the most important thing is that you seek and touch God, and let Him touch you.

When to Pray

There are many times when you will pray while fasting. Your choice of *when* to pray during a fast will be dependent upon your schedule and other factors in your life. The same is true for me. In the following section, I will tell you about how I incorporate prayer into my times of fasting. My personal approach is only a suggestion. Find the time that is best for you. The following list will give you some ideas about how to plan your prayer time when you are fasting:

- Praying during mealtime
- One special prayer time
- Praying intermittently
- Praying the Lord's Prayer
- Praying through your prayer list

Praying During Mealtime

When you are fasting, you can use mealtime for praying. This provides three times a day—breakfast, lunch and dinner—that you otherwise would not have to devote to seeking God. In the mornings, rather than going down for breakfast, I just pray in my office. During lunch, I remain in my office to read the Bible, again praying at my desk. Finally, when I come home in the evening, I return to my office and pray during the evening meal.

I have a prayer list that I pray through each day, usually in the morning. However, when I am fasting, I pray through my prayer list a second time at noon, and again at the time I'd normally eat my evening meal.

What about you? Think about ways you could replace a meal with prayer. Do whatever works well with your own schedule.

One Special Prayer Time

Try to give special (extra) time to prayer during your fast. This may mean getting up earlier in the morning, replacing normal everyday activities with prayer time, or devoting any "down time" you have to prayer.

For example, on many occasions when I travel out of town on a ministry trip, I use any extra time I have between appointments for prayer and fasting. As an illustration, I might preach in one city on the West Coast on Wednesday night and be scheduled for an appointment in a nearby location on Friday. Instead of returning to my East Coast home on Thursday, I use that extra day to fast, staying in my motel room praying and reading the Scriptures.

What opportunities do you have to devote extra time to prayer?

Praying Intermittently

Let your pangs of hunger remind you to pray. When I first started fasting, I would get twinges of hunger that reminded me of my fast. When that happened, I wanted some food, but all I did was "grin and bear it." Now when a twinge of hunger hits me, I immediately pray for the *cause* for which I am fasting.

Also, when I am fasting, I experience what I call "food temptations." Food commercials on television are more enticing than on normal days. The same is true for drive-thru windows at fast-food restaurants (even restaurants where I have never thought about eating!). When "food temptations" come, I immediately pray for my cause.

When the Bible says, "Pray without ceasing" (1 Thess. 5:17), it does not mean that we should always pray and never talk to a friend. Nor does it mean we are supposed to be in an attitude of prayer all day, every day. Our physical life negates that. When we go to a football game and our team scores, we yell and scream. Ecclesiastes says, "To everything there is a season, a time for every purpose under heaven" (3:1). When your team scores—YELL! That's not a time for a prayerful attitude.

So how can we "pray without ceasing"? The Greek word actually means to pray intermittently. Contemporary authors describe this as praying like a hacking cough that comes back on an irregular basis. We should be reminded to pray much like a cough returns again and again.

A yapping dog provides a similar illustration. I once found myself in a motel trying to sleep, but was kept awake by a yapping dog tied to a clothesline wire next to the motel. Just about the time I would get to sleep, the dog would yap and wake me up. At first I became irritated because I needed my rest for my sermon the next day. Then I remembered what the Bible means by "pray without ceasing." We are to pray intermittently. For the rest of the night, every time the dog yapped, I prayed for my sermon the next day. When you get hunger pains, pray for the cause for which you are fasting.

Praying the Lord's Prayer

Even when I am fasting I begin my day in the normal way. I set my clock for 6:00 A.M. because I always have 8:00 A.M. classes during the school year. When I awake, before I get out of bed, I pray the Lord's Prayer—not just from rote memory, but applying the Lord's Prayer to my day. I pray something like this:

> Our Father, who is in heaven and who is right
>   here in this room,

Hallowed be Thy name in this day of fasting,
Thy kingdom come through me this day,
Thy will be done in my life on earth, as Thy will
    is done in heaven,
Give me this day bread for strength so I can
    serve You,
Forgive me any sins that might disrupt my walk
    with You,
Lead me not into temptation that would cause
    me to sin,
And deliver me from the evil one who would
    destroy my walk with You.
For You have the kingdom rule,
For You have the power to answer these requests.
And you get credit for all that I ask.
    Amen.

I bounce out of the bed, put on my sweat suit and go into the kitchen to fix coffee. (No, I don't go to my desk and pray first; I want to be wide awake when I meet God, and that rush of caffeine makes me operate on all cylinders.)

After fixing my wife and myself a cup of coffee, doing some exercises, and reviewing the newspaper, I return to my desk for prayer and Bible study. There I pray the Lord's Prayer again. The Lord's Prayer prepares me for my quiet time with the Lord.

When you enter into prayer, use whatever methods help you focus on God. If you have never begun the day applying the Lord's Prayer to your own life, you may want to try it. (For more help, see *Praying the Lord's Prayer*, by Elmer Towns, Regal Books, 1998.)

Praying Through Your Prayer List

If this is your first fast, you may never have written out a prayer list. This is a good time to begin one. I've kept a prayer list since January 1951. It has several sections. You might use these sections to list the things for which you should pray.

1. *Family*. I pray daily for my wife, children, and grandchildren by name.

2. *Work Associates*. I pray for those in authority over me at my job, as well as those who work with me or in support of me. (These people are responsible for all my achievements.) I especially pray over their projects and tasks. Finally, I pray over all the work in the School of Religion where I am Dean.

3. *Church*. I pray for my pastor and the pastoral staff. I pray for my Sunday school class and the lessons I am teaching. Then I pray for the present task of my church and its ministries.

4. *Christian Leaders*. I have a list of leaders of various Christian organizations, so I pray daily for these individuals. Some are well known; some are not generally recognized. These involve evangelists, teachers, pastors, TV and radio personalities, educators, editors, publishers and counselors.

5. *Monthly Issues.* I begin a new monthly prayer list
    on the first day of each month. This is a run-
    ning list of my problems, new projects, crises,
    and the like. Items on this monthly list may
    overlap all of the items above. The monthly is-
    sues have my immediate attention.

At the end of each month, I circle the greatest answers to prayer for the last month. This becomes a time
of celebration and I usually pray, "Thank You, God, because You still answer my prayers." But more than celebration, I find this exercise has a dual kick. First, the great
answers to prayer I've seen motivate me to greater faith.
Second, some months I realize I've not had any great answers in the past thirty days. That conclusion motivates
me to a greater effort in prayer.

More on Prayer

This chapter does not completely cover the area of prayer.
No one chapter in a book could do that. There are many
outstanding books on prayer that will give you insights
and help you pray more effectively. The following list is
suggested for your reading on days when you pray:

Bounds, E. M. *Power Through Prayer*. Grand Rapids, MI:
    Baker, 1985.

Christenson, Evelyn. *What Happens When Women Pray*.
    Wheaton, IL: Victor, 1978.

Murray, Andrew. *Absolute Surrender*. Chicago, IL: Moody
    Press, 1983.

Rice, John R. *Prayer: Asking and Receiving*. Murfreesboro, TN: Sword of the Lord, 1942.

Smith, Hannah Whitall. *The Christian's Secret of a Happy Life*. Grand Rapids, MI: Fleming H. Revell, 1952.

Towns, Elmer L. *Praying the Lord's Prayer*. Ventura, CA: Regal, 1997.

Tozer, A. W. *The Pursuit of God*. Harrisburg, PA: Christian Publications, Inc., 1948.

Principles I Have Learned About Prayer and Fasting

- I pray at a higher level when I add fasting to my prayers.

- I need to plan my prayer times to be more effective in getting answers.

- I free up more time to pray when I don't eat.

- I am reminded to pray every time I feel a hunger pang when fasting.

- I will be more effective in prayer by following a prayer list.

Journaling

Begin your journal activities by writing out a prayer list. One of the advantages of keeping a journal is the habit of writing down answers you receive to prayer while fasting. Answering each of the following questions will help your journaling.

1. What did you learn about yourself when writing down your prayer list?

2. What are you learning about prayer now that you are fasting?

3. Write the greatest answer to prayer you've ever had. Why do you think God answered that prayer? What made it your greatest answer from God?

4. How did you feel when God gave you your greatest answer to prayer? Write your feelings in your journal.

5. How do you feel when a prayer is not answered? Why? Have you told God how you felt? Write your feelings in your journal.

Three-Step Bible Study

· Read the question.
· Read and analyze the Bible verse.
· Write out your response to the question.

1. How can fasting take your prayers to a higher level? Give an illustration.

"However, this kind does not go out except by prayer and fasting" (Matt. 17:21).

_____

_____

_____

_____

_____

_____

_____

_____

_____

2. Why has God not heard your prayers, nor answered
   them if you know? Give an illustration of why some of
   your prayers have not been answered.

   "If I regard iniquity in my heart, the Lord will not hear"
   (Ps. 66:18).

   *"Behold, the Lord's hand is not shortened, that it cannot
   save; nor His ear heavy, That it cannot hear. But your iniquities have separated you from your God; and your sins
   have hidden His face from you, so that He will not hear"*
   (Isa. 59:1-2).

   *"Now we know that God does not hear sinners; but if any-
   one is a worshiper of God and does His will, He hears him"*
   (John 9:31).

   _____

   _____

   _____

   _____

   _____

   _____

   _____

   _____

3. What could be another reason why God doesn't answer your prayer?

   "You do not have because you do not ask" (Jas. 4:2).

   _____

   _____

   _____

   _____

   _____

   _____

   _____

   _____

4. What is the first step to getting answers to your prayers? How will you do this?

   "Therefore I say to you, whatever things you ask when you pray, believe that you receive them, and you will have them. And whenever you stand praying, if you have anything against anyone, forgive him, that your Father in heaven may also forgive you your trespasses. But if you do not forgive, neither will your Father in heaven forgive your trespasses" (Mark 11:24-26).

   "If you abide in Me, and My words abide in you, you will ask what you desire, and it shall be done for you" (John 15:7).

   "And whatever you ask in My name, that I will do, that the Father may be glorified in the Son. If you ask anything in My name, I will do it" (John 14:13-14).

_____

_____

_____

_____

_____

_____

_____

_____

_____

_____

_____

_____

_____

5. What role does confidence have in prayer? How can you increase your confidence?

"Now this is the confidence that we have in Him, that if we ask anything according to His will, He hears us" (1 John 5:14).

_____

_____

_____

_____

_____

_____

_____

_____

_____

_____

6. Fasting is a time to call on God. What do you expect when you call on God?

"Call to Me, and I will answer you, and show you great and mighty things, which you do not know" (Jer. 33:3).

_____

_____

_____

_____

_____

_____

_____

_____

_____

_____

_____

Chapter Five

Fasting to Know God

As I was finishing a 40-day fast, a book publisher asked me, "What is the greatest answer to prayer you've received during this fast?" That question puzzled me because I had not been looking for great answers to prayer. I had joined Bill Bright in fasting for God to send revival to America. When the publisher asked me his question, I thought back to the items on my prayer list in the past 40 days. I didn't see any outstanding answers to them, so I responded, "The greatest thing is that I've gotten to know God better."

The greatest reason to fast is not to get great answers to prayer (although you may get some sensational answers). We must put first things first. The greatest benefit of fasting and prayer is that it helps us know God as never before. It helps us become quiet and focus on God so that we can recognize Him when He touches us.

God wants to reveal Himself to us, but sometimes the pressures of each day blind us to Him. One time as a teenager I was camping with two of my friends, sleeping on the ground in a tent. In the morning when we woke up, we found the footprints of deer all about our tent. We never even knew they were there during the night. In the same way, God comes to us but we don't see Him. He surrounds our tent, but the "night"—the pressures of life—eclipses His presence.

We are similar to the blind man, Bartimaeus, who sat at the gate of Jericho begging for a living. One day, as Jesus was passing through Jericho on His way to Jerusalem, Bartimaeus's life was changed. How? Bartimaeus realized that the Master was close by, that Jesus was passing near him. Maybe he overheard a conversation or maybe someone whispered to him, "Jesus is coming." No matter how the information came to him, he began to cry out, "Jesus, son of David, have mercy on me!"

Just as blind Bartimaeus yelled to get Jesus' attention, we need to cry out for God to come to us. When we are hurt or empty, we need to call to Him. The psalmist gives us some ideas of how to do it: "The sacrifices of God are a broken spirit, a broken and a contrite heart, these, O God, You will not despise" (Ps. 51:17). Through fasting, you "hunger and thirst after righteousness." You can touch the heart of God with your hungry pleas for His presence.

Picture a little baby in the arms of his mother. When the baby is hungry, he cries out for food, not caring who hears him or how much he interrupts the lives of others around him. He simply cries for food. The more you ignore the baby, the louder he cries. Oh, that we would cry out for the presence of God through fasting so that we can experience His nearness.

Have you ever cried when praying? Look again at the little baby crying out because he is hungry. Tears trickle from his innocent eyes. When is the last time you've been moved to shed tears when praying? Crying catches God's attention just as the tears of a baby let a mother know her baby needs something. And just as a mother cannot say *no* to a crying child, so God cannot say *no* to the one who cries out for His presence.

When blind Bartimaeus began to cry out for Jesus, the crowds tried to hush him. Many warned him to be quiet but he cried out all the more, "Son of David, have mercy on me!" (Mark 10:48). Perhaps the crowd was embarrassed by his shouting. Perhaps they thought he was bothering Jesus. Whatever their reason, they tried to shut up Bartimaeus but couldn't.

The blind man realized he was as close to getting healed as he would ever get. His yells told the multitude, "I refuse to let the Son of God get this close to me and then keep quiet." When you get to the place that you cannot live another day without the presence of God in your life, then fasting is easy. Giving up food is not a sacrifice, nor will you miss eating a meal. You will find the presence of God brings much greater satisfaction than food.

I'm concerned that many are not willing to pay a price to experience the presence of God. We expect God to pop up on the screen of our life, just because we are surfing the spiritual net. So, we check out the channels to "see if God is there." Like most people surfing the television, we are looking for something to tickle our fancy. But that is not the way we find God. We must want it with all of our life, so much so that we would go without food or sleep. We must be willing to sacrifice everything to experience God. We must have the attitude, *I won't quit praying until I have that presence of God.*

Pursuing God

The psalmist paints a vivid analogy of our search for God's presence in Psalm 42:1: "As the deer pants for the water brooks, so pants my soul for You, O God." Here is a picture of the young deer, probably chased by dogs or other predators, frantically running to escape. Because the deer is tired and thirsty, it is searching for refreshment, a running creek or stream where it can take a drink of water. Like the deer, we are in need of refreshment, searching to drink deeply from heaven's cup, remembering the promise of Jesus: "He who comes to Me shall never hunger, and he who believes in Me shall never thirst" (John 6:35).

When you fast you stop pursuing food and the other necessities of life to passionately pursue the presence of God. The trouble is, spiritual passion has become "politically incorrect." Christians don't want to be called religious fanatics, or even worse, "religious nuts." The world tells us we should quietly meditate on God. The crowd tells us it is incorrect to weep, to lift our hands in prayer or to beg God for His presence.

Remember, God has never done away with the idea of sacrifice. Just as God taught Old Testament believers the necessity of offering an animal sacrifice because they sinned, so God would have us bring sacrifices when we come to worship Him. True, the sacrifice for our sin is the blood of Jesus Christ, and it has already been made. We are accepted by God because "the blood of Jesus Christ His Son cleanses us from all sin" (1 John 1:7).

But there is another type of sacrifice we need to bring after we are saved: the sacrifice of our worship and praise. Hebrews 13 explains this of New Testament believers: "We have an altar from which those who serve the tabernacle [i.e., the worship center in the Old Testament] have no right to eat.... Therefore, let us go forth to Him [Jesus], outside the camp. . . . let us continually offer the sacrifice of praise to God, that is, the fruit of our lips, giving thanks to His name" (vv. 10,13,15).

Remember, God sees the hungry when they call out to Him and does something about it. We are promised, "Delight yourself also in the Lord, and He shall give you the desires of your heart" (Ps. 37:4). God is not interested in providing His food for those who just want to nibble around the edges. God reveals Himself to those who eat fully from His table.

Suppose God does come to visit your life. Suppose you've experienced spending a few minutes in prayer and God has spoken to you. The question is, does He stay? Do you have a hard time keeping the presence of God in your life? When we learn to worship Him, He stays around to enjoy our worship. A habit of worship makes God feel welcome all the time instead of just in your morning watch.

Tommy Tenney, in his book *The God Chasers,* tells the story of a very heavy Christian worker who had trouble finding a chair big enough to sit in when he went to visit others in their homes. When he entered a room, he surveyed the chairs to see if they were strong enough to hold him. Tenney said that his friend was so large and had broken so many chairs that he just visited people in the front hall.

In the same way, does God come into our life looking for a chair that is prepared for Him, but leave because we haven't prepared a place? Unless we prepare a place for God in our heart, His presence will not stay with us. When God finds a heart that is earnestly seeking Him, God will come and stay with that person.

Years ago in the movie *Field of Dreams*, the key phrase stated, *"If you build it, he will come."* In the same way, if you build a resting place for God in your heart, He will come to dwell with you.

Worshiping God

Where can we find God? Of course, God is everywhere present all the time. But we don't always see Him or experience His presence. Sometimes, because things are so difficult and we hurt so deeply we think God is nowhere to be found. So how can we experience the presence of God in our lives?

God comes to those who worship Him. "But You are holy, Enthroned in the praises of Israel" (Ps. 22:3). Because God seeks our worship, He responds to us when we worship Him.

Paul and Silas were arrested for preaching the gospel in Philippi. They had cast a demon out of the young servant girl. The demon had helped the young girl tell fortunes, so when Paul and Silas hurt the fortune-telling business, the girl's owner had them arrested. Paul and Silas were cast into prison—but not just a cell; the jailer "put them into the inner prison and fastened their feet in the stocks" (Acts 16:24). Paul and Silas had tried simply to do the will of God, and they were persecuted, beaten, and now shackled in stocks.

Probably none of us have ever been beaten because of our faith in Christ. Probably none of us will ever be thrown into prison and have our feet shackled. Usually when something like this happens to us we complain or begin justifying ourselves. Not Paul and Silas. "At midnight, Paul and Silas were praying and singing praises unto God" (Acts 16:25). Since God comes to those who worship and praise Him, what happened? Notice the use of the words "suddenly" and "immediately" indicate how quickly God came to them: "*Suddenly* there was a great earthquake, so that the foundations of the prison were shaken; and *immediately* all the doors were opened and everyone's chains were loosed" (Acts 16:26, emphasis mine). If you want the presence of God to come into your life, worship and praise Him. God will come to you as He came to Paul and Silas in prison. You may not feel the earthquake, but if you are searching, you will feel His presence.

Not only did the earthquake free Paul and Silas, but also all of the other prisoners were freed. This is a picture of all that happens when we worship God: He sets the captives free. If you are bound in sin and bad habits, try praising God to experience His presence and power. Power comes with God's presence. When God visited the jail in Philippi, an earthquake opened all the doors. Was that to let Paul and Silas out or to let God in?

You may face many blocks that keep you from doing God's will. While you should be free in Jesus, you find yourself bound in stocks. Sometimes your bondage is emotional; at other times it is spiritual. Perhaps you need physical healing. In any case, what should you do? In the middle of the night, Paul and Silas did not complain nor were they consoling one another. Because they sang praises, God visited the jail. Don't look at your shackles; sing praises so that you can usher the presence of God into your circumstances.

I once met an elderly saint who had learned to praise God in trials and problems. No matter what went wrong in his life, he thanked God that it wasn't worse than it was, that it was "only a little problem." He would say, "Everyone has problems. God is good because He gives me little problems and not big problems." He saw the mercy of God in his problems. Do you?

I believe the world is searching for God, more than we realize. The problem is that, when they look into the Church, they see only people with problems, failures, sins and weaknesses. If the Church could learn to worship God in everything, including problems, the eyes of the world might see Jesus more often.

When the world looks at us, what do they see? They don't see Christ because we are not worshiping Him. All they see are people doing their religious duties. Too often, they focus on our humanness and never see God's presence. By this, I don't mean that Christians should be overly focused on what the world sees. Not at all. Rather, we should seek the heart of God so that we may gain the presence of God. Then others might see Him more clearly. And we should lose our fear of what people think of us and become concerned about what God thinks of us.

Being Intimate with God

One of the most amazing stories in the Old Testament was Absalom, the son of David who had difficulty getting into the throne room to see his father. Because of Absalom's previous sin, he had run away from his father. Eventually though, Absalom came back to the city of Jerusalem, but even then, there was no reconciliation. "And Absalom dwelt two full years in Jerusalem, but did not see the king's face" (2 Sam. 14:28). He was in the city, but could not visit his father in the throne room. Is it possible to be in the king's city and not see his face? Is it possible to pray to God but not experience His presence?

Many Christians live second-rate spiritual lives because of a past sin or failure. Something in the past has blocked their fellowship with God. Perhaps it was a disobedience. In any case, they go to church but don't experience the presence of God; they pray daily but don't experience the heart of God.

My pastor says he must experience the heart of God in fellowship before he can experience the hand of God in answered prayer. Instead of praying, "Bless me," he spends time praising God and "blessing Him." Is the whole time we spend in prayer asking, "Give to me," when we should learn, "God, I give to You"?

When my children were small, I would come home from a trip with presents for them. If they didn't meet me at the airport, they surely met me at the front door with the question, "What did you bring me?" I used to tell them, "My own sweet self." I thought that was a cute answer, but they didn't. They wanted their gifts. In the same way, many people come to God looking for His "presents" rather than looking for His "presence." They are more interested in gifts than they are in the giver.

My wife taught the children to be grateful. As soon as they got their gifts they hugged me and kissed me. Then, I knew everything was all right. When they told me, "I love you," I determined I would bring more gifts next time.

Likewise, I love my grandchildren and love to give them gifts, too. During Christmas 1999, a Mennonite farmer who had seen my Bible class on TV made a small solid table and two chairs as a gift to my grandchildren for Christmas. One chair was for Collyn and the other for Brad. At Christmas dinner we let the children sit at their small table while the adults sat at the big table. Little Collyn later requested of me, "Sit with me." It was a sturdy little chair and here was big "Doc" (the grandchildren call me Doc) sitting in the little chair with my knees high in the air, enjoying dessert—ice cream and cake—with my granddaughter.

I think that's the way God visits us at times. We are so small and God is so magnificent, but He delights to visit His children, to sit on their chairs, and then have "dessert" with them. When is the last time you've asked God to come sit in fellowship with you while you enjoyed dessert?

We have perfected the art of entertaining people in our home. We know how to make them feel comfortable, how to feed them and how to entertain them. But what about God? Have we practiced the art of entertaining God in our lives? Just as we meet people at the front door to invite them into our homes, do we know how to invite God into our lives? If you bring God into your life, do you know where He can sit? Have you learned how to praise God and how to worship Him? Most of us only run into His presence to seek His hand in answer to prayer, and then leave to be about our daily business. But we must go beyond seeking His hand; we must seek His heart.

When a young man asks his sweetheart for her hand in marriage, obviously he wants more than her hand. Since the hand symbolizes the heart, we begin with the hand. A young man begins by holding the woman's hand long before there is a kiss and embrace. The hand is only the first step of intimacy, both in a marriage relationship as well as in our spiritual relationship to God. We must go beyond asking for things from His hand and fall in love with His heart.

Let's examine that statement more carefully. There are two ways to know God. First, when you come to know God in salvation, that is a "once for all" commitment that gives you eternal life. But, there is a second way to know God. It is becoming intimate with Him every day. Much like marriage, you meet that first time and you learn to know him or her. But after marriage you learn to know your spouse in a deeper way, and no matter how long you live, you never fully know one another. It becomes a growing, lifelong experience.

Knowing God is a daily task. Jesus said, "If anyone desires to come after Me, let him deny himself, and take up his cross daily, and follow Me" (Luke 9:23). Note that Jesus said *daily*. You did not decide to follow Him for just one time or one day, but on an ongoing basis. In the same way you can make fasting a continuous practice in your life. (I fast one day each week.) You may be preparing for your first fast; don't let it be your last. You will want to fast many times as a way of following God daily.

This may not be limited to giving up food only. It may mean giving up other things, such as recreation or relaxation, your time or your money, or the pursuit of any other pleasure in your life. Be willing to follow God daily by putting these things behind you in order to seek the presence of Christ. He is waiting for you to find Him.

Principles I Learned About Knowing God

· I can know God through fasting.

· When I am searching for God, He is waiting for me to find Him.

· If I really want to know God, I must search for Him with all my body and soul.

· If I prepare a place for God's presence, He will come to me.

· I seek God's presence for Himself, not the blessings that He gives.

Journaling

As you fast and seek to know God, write down what you see, hear, feel and experience. Answer the following questions to guide your journal entries.

1. How do you feel when you search for God and can't find Him? How have you been searching for God before this fast?

2. Blind Bartimaeus cried out for Jesus. Describe how you have cried out for God. What was God's response?

3. How has fasting from earthly food helped you seek and find God?

4. What do you need to do to prepare a place for God to come "sit" in your life? List some suggestions.

5. Paul and Silas cried out in spite of the shackles. List the "shackles" that are presently binding you. Write a letter to God telling how you will praise Him in spite of your shackles.

Three-Step Bible Study

· Read the question.
· Read and analyze the Bible verse.
· Write out your response to the question.

1. The word "know" is used two ways in Scripture. In the first place it means to know God in salvation; and second, it means to know God in fellowship or communion with Him (intimacy). What type of knowledge do you need for salvation?

"This is eternal life, that they may know You, the only true God, and Jesus Christ whom You have sent" (John 17:3).

"These things I have written to you who believe in the name of the Son of God, that you may know that you have eternal life, and that you may continue to believe in the name of the Son of God" (1 John 5:13).

"Not everyone who says to Me, 'Lord, Lord,' shall enter the kingdom of heaven, but he who does the will of My Father in heaven. Many will say to Me in that day, 'Lord, Lord, have we not prophesied in Your name, cast out demons in Your name, and done many wonders in Your name?' And then I will declare to them, 'I never knew you; depart from Me, you who practice lawlessness!'" (Matt. 7:21-23).

_____

_____

_____

_____

_____

_____

_____

2. There is a second way to know God intimately. The Scriptures below describe the passion of the apostle Paul and the psalmist David. How have you expressed this passion?

"That I may know Him and the power of His resurrection, and the fellowship of His sufferings, being conformed to His death" (Phil. 3:10).

"As the deer pants for the water brooks, so pants my soul for You, O God. When shall I come and appear before God? My tears have been my food day and night, while they continually say to me, where is your God?" (Ps. 42:1-3).

_____

_____

_____

_____

_____

_____

_____

3. Once you know God and His Son, Jesus Christ, what must you do to be happy? Give two illustrations of how you will carry this out today.

"If you know these things, blessed are you if you do them" (John 13:17).

_____

_____

_____

_____

_____

_____

4. How did David respond to the invitation by God to seek God's face? Write some ways you will seek God.

"When You said, 'Seek My face,' my heart said to You, 'Your face, Lord, I will seek.' Do not hide Your face from me; do not turn Your servant away in anger; You have been my help; do not leave me nor forsake me, O God of my salvation" (Ps. 27:8-9).

_____

_____

_____

_____

_____

_____

_____

5. What time of day is suggested that you seek God? Write what you will do with your schedule to apply this verse.

"O God, You are my God; early will I seek You; my soul thirsts for You; my flesh longs for You in a dry and thirsty

land where there is no water. So I have looked for You in the sanctuary" (Ps. 63:1-2).

"Evening, and morning, and at noon, I will pray, and cry aloud: and he shall hear my voice" (Ps. 55:17).

_____

_____

_____

_____

_____

_____

_____

6. What are some of the results that God promises to those who seek God? Write some things God has done for you because you sought the Lord.

"I waited patiently for the Lord; and He inclined to me, and heard my cry. He also brought me up out of a horrible pit, out of the miry clay, and set my feet upon a rock, and established my steps. He has put a new song in my mouth, praise to our God: many will see it and fear, and will trust in the Lord. Blessed is that man that makes the Lord his trust, and does not respect the proud, nor such as turn aside to lies" (Ps. 40:1-4).

_____

_____

_____

_____

_____

_____

Chapter Six

Fasting to Wait on God

Everyone has problems. You don't have to be a terrible sinner to get into trouble. Normal people have days when they don't know what to do. Some days you may not know which way to turn and tomorrow may look fuzzy.

When the dark days come, remember to fast and pray. Why fast? To wait on God. When you are praying, fasting and waiting, you are putting yourself in a position where God can help you. God is always there for you, but when you fast, God comes to help solve your problem.

> They that wait upon the Lord shall renew their stamina, even when things go wrong. They can fly over problems like an eagle mounting up with wings. They shall run and not be weary of the journey; they shall walk and not faint (Isa. 40:31, author's translation).

Do you need "wings" to fly up over a discouraging situation? Next time your problems get you discouraged, think about "wings." God may have some wings to deliver you.

There are two kinds of people who need wings. First there are the devastated persons—those drained of energy. Usually these people have given up in life. They're not looking for anything, especially not for wings to get them back on their feet. They're so devastated by some circumstances that they can't see anything but the problems that got them into a hole. If you're devastated, fast so that God can give you a desire for wings.

There's another type of person who needs wings. These people are not discouraged; instead, they're fighting, trying, struggling to get off the ground. To the person who's frantically searching, take time to fast and wait on God. He can give you wings to get airborne.

The Wings You Need

The cry for wings is as old as mankind. Because people have always had problems, they have always wanted to fly away. Some people live in addictive prisons of their own making or behind circumstantial bars made by someone else. Hardly knowing what to dream, the human spirit frets over its shackles; it cries for deliverance; it prays for wings. You may be able to relate to this. Because you long to "fly away" from a hateful prison, because you are made in God's image, because you want a better life, because you want to soar, here's what you must do: wait, fast, and pray for wings to fly up and away.

Are you looking in the wrong place for wings? Some people look in a whiskey glass or drugs. Some try to find it in sex. But none of those are the right place to find your wings. Look again at the promise: "They that wait upon the Lord . . . shall mount up with wings as eagles." The wings are found by waiting in God's presence, and the best place to start is with a fast.

God has the wings you need; He knows where they are hidden. When you wait on God, He'll tell you where to find the solutions to your problems. He knows when circumstances will turn around, or He may lead you directly to your answer. He may show you your wings through something else in your life, like your church, or your bank, or a new job. But He doesn't always do it directly. God may tell a friend where your wings are hiding and your friend can help you find them.

Sometimes God gives the wings to your spouse. He wants you to get in harmony with the most important person in your life, so He may first help your marriage before He helps you fly over your problems.

At other times God keeps wings hidden for a long time. He knows where they are, but He doesn't tell you. God wants you to search for them because searching will develop your character, your faith, or your dependence on Him. In the final analysis, searching for wings will teach you many things.

Today you may be walking wearily through your trouble, not even looking to God for an answer. You weep for a season, you struggle for a season, and you complain a lot. You've tried to solve your problems. You have even cried out, "Doesn't God care? Where is God?"

Yes, God cares! He is right where He's always been. He is waiting for you where you last saw Him. He wants you to slow down so you can hear Him. He wants you to come to Him. It's in God's presence that you will learn what God wants to teach you. Then, He can give you wings to mount up like an eagle.

You can be happy, regain your excitement, and even feel the awesome presence of the Lord again. Just wait on God. First, seek His presence; second, wait on His direction;

third, mount up with wings He supplies; and fourth, soar over problems.

What are these wings that I've been speaking of?

Wings are answers you find in the presence of God. For you, a wing may be "repentance." You may need to quit doing something you know is wrong, and repent for it. Is your family in trouble because of a secret, cancerous sin that saps your strength? Maybe you've been hiding your spiritual cancer. Most people are embarrassed to confess they have cancer, so they don't tell anyone, not even God. If this describes you, let the Great Physician cut out that cancer. You can get healthy and you can fly again. Your family can get well, too. New wings can lift you out of your trouble. Repent. Tell God you're sorry. Wait on God. If you'll let God work through you now like He did in the past, He will provide wings to fly you over this obstacle.

How do we begin to fly? Slowly.

An eagle doesn't take off like a rocket. Even when you first fly with God's wings, it'll be slow going at first. Wounded people walk slowly.

Beginning to fly over your problems may not be easy. Notice the great energy in an eagle's wings as he takes off. The eagle gives all his strength to lift himself off the ground. There is sound, the flapping of wings, furious activity, and then he flies. Compare this initial burst of energy to the effortless flight once the eagle reaches the higher air currents. Like the eagle's flight, waiting on God may be hard at first; "mounting up with eagle's wings" may be difficult, but it will work and it is worth the effort.

You will need two wings: the first wing is called *vision* to see the future through God's eyes. Scripture says, "Without a vision the people perish" (Prov. 29:18).

The second wing is called *courage*. You need to act on what God shows you. Remember what God said to Joshua: "Only be strong and courageous, that you may observe and do all the principles of God" (Josh. 1:7).

The first flap of the wings is the hardest! The first time you fast may be the hardest. When you're hurting, it's hard to wait. It's hard for a drowning person to stop struggling. But wait, set God at the center of your life, fast, and pray.

When you wait upon the Lord, you'll be lifted into the sky. When your wings stretch out to the heavens, you'll feel the surge of air lifting you over your obstacles.

For those of you who jump into action first and seek God later, remember that jumping is not flying. Some people try to jump over their problems. They back up to get a running start, thinking, *The faster I run, the farther I'll jump*. They attempt to leap over their barriers with self-efforts, to solve their problems in their own way. The secret, they say, is trying hard enough. But remember, jumping doesn't release you from the law of gravity. When you jump you will always come down.

People tend to jump into action to solve a present problem the same way they have jumped in the past. But there comes a time when you can no longer jump. The problem is too big, too high, too complex, too serious. The obstacle is too high to jump over.

Maybe, this time, you have even forgotten how to jump. You've broken a leg, you're too old, or you're too weak to jump. Is someone holding you back so that you can't jump? Maybe you're at a place where the self-effort you have used in the past doesn't work anymore. What can you do when you can't jump?

Fly!

"They that wait on the Lord . . . shall mount up with wings of eagles" (Isa. 40:31). The soul is not crushed by the problems of earth if it has wings to fly over them. The dreams of the heart are not imprisoned behind bars if the heart has wings to soar over its barriers.

Think again of the eagle. How can its wings break the power of gravity? As the eagle's wings reach to heaven, the sky is pulled into its breast, and then the eagle automatically is lifted into the heaven it seeks. When you reach up to heaven, it automatically pulls dreams into your heart. When you reach up to God, you are pulling Him into your experience. Your wings lift you up from the ground, and each reach of the wing takes you higher. Wings lift you up over your problems, as you pull God down into your circumstances.

As your wings continually reach for heaven, you fly higher. The ground and gravity lose their hold over you. The higher you fly, the less hold the things of this world have upon you. Your wings give you freedom.

Waiting Upon God

As you wait upon God, He gives you wings to fly over your burdens. Problems may not go away immediately, just as the first reach of the wings doesn't propel the eagle into the heaven of heavens. But slowly, with each reach of the wing, the eagle rises higher. Slowly, each time you retreat to God's presence, you look at things differently. You slowly gain strength—just as each day of exercise strengthens the body. You can overcome the deepest financial debt, one day at a time, one bill at a time. Gradually, you can come out of the deepest and blackest pit, solving one problem at a time.

The higher a bird flies, the less pull gravity has upon it. For you, the more you mount up with "wings as eagles," the less you'll want to return to the old ways. If you go high enough, you'll experience no gravity at all. Like astronauts, you'll float, free and unrestricted. The gravity pull of sin and deviousness will lose its hold over you.

No one reaches spiritual maturity in one day. As we wait on God, learn about Him, follow Him and talk to Him, we become like Him. Sin like gravity has less hold on us. So waiting in the presence of God can teach us to live above our circumstances and above our trials. But, what must we do to get started?

"Mount up."

The greatest wings are useless, unless used. A bird can't lift himself with its wings if they are not spread. You can't fly if your wings don't reach for the heavens. If the bird doesn't attempt to pull heaven down, it doesn't fly upward. The secret to flying: "Mount up with wings."

Begin today. Don't stay in your discouragement. Don't try to jump over your problems with self-effort. Wait on God, fast, pray. Find out what God would have you do, and then mount up. The way to fly is to wait on the Lord. In His presence there is an answer to solve your problems.

You have to wait to get wings.

When I was a little boy, waiting was hard to do. I was impatient. I wanted everything—NOW! Most of us are impatient. We want God to solve our problems—NOW! We even pray for God to solve our problems—NOW! We don't say it in audible words, but our hearts mean it when we pray, "HURRY!" But God's way is to wait. The answer is often slower, not faster.

A halfhearted commitment to waiting is not enough. Have you ever seen someone fidget while standing in line? The line doesn't move fast enough for them so they fidget and stew. You can't stew in God's presence. You can't hurry God; you must wait on God. Fidgeting in God's presence will not help you fly.

Have you ever watched two people who are in love? They enjoy spending time with each other. Neither looks at a watch; they are eager to remain in the other's presence. They are not uncomfortable with one another. It takes this kind of commitment when waiting on God. Become consumed with His presence. Give Him your total attention. You can't be worried about your problems and then get anything out of the presence of God.

Flying in Faith

No bird ever gets off the ground by passively flapping its wings. No! It takes a bird's total commitment to fly. The bird must commit everything to flight. You will not "mount up" if you lazily seek God or halfheartedly try to fly.

Flying is total commitment.

The bird on the tree limb leaps out into empty space, trusting its wings. The bird knows what its wings will do because it has flown before. It takes a total leap into the air. Notice, the bird does two things at the same time. First, the bird leaps out into nothing, trusting the air to sustain it. Second, the bird spreads its wings into heaven and its wings begin to lift it into the sky. Each time the eagle reaches its wings toward God, it flies higher and higher. The bird must do two things: it must leap and it must reach.

The leap of the bird from the limb is similar to our yielding ourselves to God. To yield means to surrender. Yield your circumstances to God. Let go of the security of the tree limb. Bring your problems into God's presence and "wait upon the Lord." Make sure you leave them there. Do not pick them up and try to carry them away. In His presence learn what you must do about your problems.

To "mount up with wings of eagles," you must leave the security of your past habits and practices. Today, you may find your security in keeping up a good image, or in lying about your accomplishments, or in "fudging the numbers," or in giving a "spin" to your side of the story.

But to get God's answer, you must yield the way you have solved your problems in the past. You must yield your past way of thinking and your past way of doing business. You must yield everything—or surrender yourself—to God.

Give everything to God—your past, your failure, your problems, your future—everything.

Flying is another word for exercising faith. Faith is leaping off the tree limb, reaching your wings to heaven, pulling heaven down and lifting yourself up from the pull of gravity. Faith is gliding on the air. Faith is repeating the action over and over because one flap of the wings is not enough. After you take one giant leap in faith, you must continually fly in faith.

Faith is applying God's principles to your problem. Faith is first asking God, "What would You have me do?" then doing it. Faith would ask God a second question: "What would You do for me?" Then letting Him do it.

Unused wings die! If a bird doesn't exercise its wings, they will gradually wither, becoming useless. If you had nothing in your life that forced you to fly—your problems—you might lose your ability to fly and your desire to fly. Sometimes, God pushes you out of the nest to develop your wings; at other times He makes the nest so uncomfortable you are forced to leap out and develop your wings.

As you look at your problems, you tend to think how big, how gruesome, how painful they are. But there is another problem that's even more awful: the problem of useless wings. What would happen if you couldn't fly with your wings?

That would be like being in a flock of birds feeding in the fresh spring grass, when suddenly a cat—a predator looking to kill and steal—sneaks up. The birds would scatter in flight, except for one. With useless wings, the threat of the cat would be magnified for the bird unable to fly.

We all have enemies. There's usually someone who doesn't like us. We know that our enemy, the devil, is always sneaking about like a roaring lion that wants to devour us. Our enemies may build traps to catch us, but God gives us wings to deliver us.

Our enemies can build walls as high as they please and padlock us as tightly as possible, but there is no prison that can hold us as long as we keep the way open between us and God. If we "mount up with wings," we can fly higher than any of their walls can reach.

God may push you out of the nest because He knows there will be dark stormy days ahead. He may push you out of the nest to strengthen your wings. He may know you'll need strong wings to make it through a coming storm to the other side.

If you need some encouragement, look at the word "shall." "They that wait upon the Lord, *shall* renew their strength, they *shall* mount up with wings." God didn't say, "You *may* mount up with wings." The only part of the promise that has a condition is the "waiting." You have to wait upon the Lord. If you wait upon the Lord, you *shall* mount up with wings.

To "mount up with wings" is not giving in because you can't do anything else. "Mount up" is power and action. When God says "mount up," think of cowboys "mounting up their horses." Think of soldiers launching a charge against the enemy.

God tells you to "mount up with wings as an eagle." Notice He directs you to one of the most powerful of all birds. He doesn't want you on sparrow's wings, or butterfly wings, or even the wings of a dove—but eagle's wings. The eagle is among the fastest, strongest and most powerful birds. So when you think of eagles, think strength!

To be strong, wait in God's presence and fast and pray. Then take action in faith.

Principles I Learned by Waiting and Fasting

- I get strength to do difficult things when I fast and wait before the Lord.

- I can endure any problem or persecution when I fast and wait before the Lord.

- I get new strength that I didn't know I had when I fast and wait before the Lord.

- I am able to soar on eagle's wings over enemies, situations and attacks after fasting and prayer.

- I can keep on doing the difficult things required of me after I fast and wait on God.

Journaling

Write about situations where you have had to wait on God because there were no other alternatives. Use the following questions to direct what to write in your journal.

1. What were some difficult situations where you had no alternative but to wait on God? Why were they difficult? Why couldn't you run away? How did you feel?

2. What were some times when God came near to help you through difficult situations? How did you seek God? How did God help you wait?

3. How did God give you inner strength in difficult times? What did you experience?

4. The Bible describes how you can "mount up with wings of eagles." How did eagle's wings help you overcome problems? How did you "walk"? "Run"?

5. What will you do in the future when difficulties come? What will you do to "fly" over your difficulties and barriers?

Three-Step Bible Study

· Read the question.
· Read and analyze the Bible verse.
· Write out your response to the question.

1. The Bible tells you to wait on Him. What is the greatest thing you get by waiting?

   "Truly my soul silently [waits] for God; From Him [comes] my salvation" (Ps. 62:1).

   _____

   _____

   _____

   _____

   _____

   _____

   _____

2. Give some personal reasons why you should wait upon the Lord.

"Be sober, be vigilant; because your adversary the devil walks about like a roaring lion, seeking whom he may devour" (1 Pet. 5:8).

_____

_____

_____

_____

_____

_____

3. What are some things you can do when waiting on God?

"Praying always with all prayer and supplication in the Spirit, being watchful to this end with all perseverance and supplication for all the saints" (Eph. 6:19).

"Continue earnestly in prayer, being vigilant in it with thanksgiving" (Col. 4:2).

_____

_____

_____

_____

_____

_____

_____

_____

4. What strength is available to help you overcome temptation by waiting on God?

"No temptation has overtaken you except such as is common to man; but God [is] faithful, who will not allow you to be tempted beyond what you are able, but with the temptation will also make the way of escape, that you may be able to bear it" (1 Cor. 10:13).

_____

_____

_____

_____

_____

_____

5. When you wait on God, what happens inside you?

"Be anxious for nothing, but in everything by prayer and supplication, with thanksgiving, let your requests be made known to God; and the peace of God, which surpasses all understanding, will guard your hearts and minds through Christ Jesus" (Phil. 4:6-7).

_____

_____

_____

_____

_____

_____

6. What is the negative thing you must avoid when walking with God?

"[There is] therefore now no condemnation to those who are in Christ Jesus, who do not walk according to the flesh, but according to the Spirit" (Rom. 8:1).

_____

_____

_____

_____

_____

_____

_____

_____

_____

Chapter Seven

Fasting When You're Scared

Sometimes in life you are scared—scared silly, scared out of your wits. You feel like you're running, but a *death shadow* is catching up with you, biting at your heels; surely it will pounce on you, and then you'll die.

I remember watching a *National Geographic* television program in which a tiger was chasing down an antelope. The antelope ran frantically, cutting sharply to the right then to the left, to elude the tiger. The faster antelope should have outrun the tiger, but each time the antelope cut sharply, the tiger quickly recovered its steps and went bounding after it.

As I watched, I kept hoping and praying that the antelope would escape; I breathed a sigh of relief each time the antelope put a little distance between it and the predator. But the antelope didn't escape. Finally, with one gigantic leap, the antelope was knocked to the ground, and before it could regain its feet, the tiger locked its powerful jaws in a death grip on the neck of the antelope.

Once the antelope was caught, I thought my emotions would subside. But no! The TV camera zoomed in on the eyes of the antelope. I saw fear, terror, approaching death in the antelope's eyes. The tiger kept resetting its teeth grips into the neck of the antelope. Now it was impossible to run away. The antelope was still alive, but dying from its death wound. It was being eaten alive.

Do you ever feel like an antelope being pursued by your enemy? Is your enemy catching up? Is he going to eat you alive?

Sometimes we come to a fast not to get an answer to prayer, not to intimately know God, and not even to worship the Lord. We come to God in fasting because we are scared and there is nothing else to do but fast.

The word "fast" comes from the Hebrew word *tsom*, which means to afflict yourself. When a crisis comes, you don't have to discipline yourself not to eat; you lose your appetite because something is threatening you. You are afflicted. You don't want food simply because you're scared to death and focused on the thing that scares you.

Suppose you receive a message that your spouse or child has been in a terrible automobile accident. As you rush to the hospital, you notice it's noon—lunchtime. You wouldn't think of pulling through a fast-food drive-thru lane to get a hamburger. The threat to your loved one would consume all your attention. Food would not be important. Fasting is a natural response when we are scared.

Perhaps the Scripture that deals with fear best is Psalm 23. Here is my paraphrased version:

> The Lord is my Shepherd, I shall not want any
> thing. . . .
> Even when walking through a valley of dangers,
> I will not be scared of *death shadows*,
> Because You are with me (Ps. 23:1,4, author's
> translation).

If you haven't read Psalm 23 recently, take time to read it now. It describes believers as sheep and the Lord as our Shepherd. Of all the animals created, sheep are one of the most vulnerable to danger. They aren't cunning enough to take care of themselves and they have no weapons of defense. A crab has claws, a wolf has fangs, a snake can bite, and a skunk can ward off danger by stinking up its surroundings. But sheep are defenseless. They depend on a shepherd for protection from danger.

Sheep by nature are not watchful, either, often making them oblivious to danger. They wander too close to the edge of a cliff and topple over. They roam too far into deep water and are drowned or are carried away in a swift current. They put their heads into the grass to eat, never looking up or listening for danger around them because they are too busy feeding their appetites. They watch neither for poisonous serpents, wolves, nor any other predator lurking in caves nearby.

Isn't that like us? We are busy feeding our appetites on television, on recreation, or at the fast-food places. We are busy satisfying ourselves on all that the world has to offer. We rarely look up as long as there is plenty of pleasure to feed on. Are we not oblivious to the dangerous New Age trends in the cartoons that our children watch? Do we even see dangers in the sexual innuendoes in the movies and television programs that entertain us? We forget that Satan is a *roaring lion*.

As the Lord's sheep, you need to lift your head from feeding yourself and be aware of the dangers around you. You need to look up—look to God to protect you. There are two things you can do when you are threatened. First, take time to fast, and second, retreat to the quiet presence of God. The Shepherd will receive you and protect you. Cut yourself off from physical food so that you can look to God for spiritual food and protection. When in danger, try fasting.

Death Shadows

What's scaring you today? Maybe your problem is not your real problem. Many things that frighten us never happen, and our greatest fear is fear itself. Are you scared of shadows? Are you afraid of what might happen? The psalmist said he would not be afraid of *death shadows* when walking through dark valleys.

Remember as a child when your mom put you to bed and you were frightened by the threatening shadows creeping into your bedroom? Maybe a shadow was formed by a light under the door, or from a night-light or from a streetlight; whatever its source, you were afraid of the shadows cast on the wall by the faint rays of light that crept into your bedroom. Remember trying to put your head under the covers, but every time you peeked out the *death shadow* was there? The more you stared at your scary shadow, the more you were positive you saw it move and that it was always coming to get you!

Now we laugh at our childhood fears, but they were real to us when we were children. Don't forget we are children of God who are scared of the shadows of this world. Just as a small child cries out to Dad when awakened from a scary dream, cry out to your heavenly Father when you are afraid.

What shadow is stealing joy from your life? Is it the shadow of financial ruin because you're afraid you won't have enough money when you retire? Or maybe you can't pay the first-of-the-month bills. Or maybe—*whoosh*—an unplanned medical emergency has drained away your savings. Is the shadow that scares you a little nagging pain that you think might be cancer?

Some shadows are so big that just the thought of them scares us to death. Often if we are able to dismiss them for days or even weeks, we will again feel the hot breath of the *death shadows* on the backs of our necks and think we only have moments to live.

Remember God's invitation: "Call unto me in the day of trouble: I will deliver thee" (Ps. 50:15).

When shadows scare you, take time to fast and seek God's presence. There is no darkness in God's presence, nor is there any shadow. Jesus said, "I am the light of the world and he that followeth me shall not walk in darkness" (John 8:12). Fasting can bring light to your night. It will help you hear again the promise of the twenty-third Psalm: "Thou art with me."

Even if you are walking through your personal "valley of the shadow of death," remember what the psalmist says: "Yea though I walk *through* the valley. . . ." God promises you will walk *through* the valley. Not just *into* the valley to be left there, but all the way *through* it. God never abandons you in the valley, nor does He stay outside the valley while you are in it. He promises to go *with* you *through* your trouble. God's name *Immanuel* means "God with us."

When your finances collapse, remember Immanuel. When you go to find out the results of your cancer test, remember Immanuel. Remember Immanuel for little problems and for terrifying ones.

This doesn't mean evil will not hit you: you may have cancer, your company may go bankrupt, a loved one may die. The psalmist says, "I will fear no evil"; he doesn't say, "I will experience no evil." Neither does he say, "God will keep evil from me because He is with me"; rather, he says, "When evil comes, I will not fear it because God walks with me through it." God is with me when *death shadows* scare me.

The most amazing image in Psalm 23 is what we see after we exit the valley of the shadow of death. We see a meal—a banquet—that the Shepherd has prepared for us in the presence of our enemies (see v. 5). Usually when we are running from danger we never think about eating a meal. All we think about is getting away from the predator that is dogging our footsteps. We think about running to some safeguarded spot, climbing a tree that *death shadows* can't climb, hiding in a protective castle where *death shadows* can't penetrate. We seek security and comfort. So what does God do to make us feel confident and victorious? He prepares a table overflowing with food for us. We don't end up hiding up a tree fearing for our lives, nor crouching behind a castle wall. Because the Lord is our Shepherd, we can sit down to eat in the presence of our enemies.

Has God fixed a good, hot meal for you lately? Let me tell you how it's done. When you fast from this world's food, God prepares a spiritual table for you. Come, sit in His presence, and eat His food.

Psalm 78 describes Israel's desperate conditions in the wilderness. The nation had disobeyed God and refused to enter into the Promised Land for fear of the "giants." The people were relegated to 40 years of wandering in the wilderness until all of the adults over 20 years old died. As the Israelites wandered in the wilderness, they continued in unbelief, asking, "Can God spread a table in the desert?" (Ps. 78:19).

That is the question we ask. When I am scared to death—too scared to eat—can God feed me? Can He spread a table in *my* wilderness? When I feel great, imminent danger, can I ever be secure again? What is the answer? "My cup overflows" (Ps. 23:5). God does not give us a mere squirt of water from a plastic bottle as though we were a boxer between rounds or a marathon runner getting a quick refresher as he frantically dashes on. No. When we are scared, God's provision will cause us to say, "My cup overflows."

Get your attitude toward God right and ask Him to walk through your danger with you. If you trust Him, He will take away your fear of the shadows. Remember, shadows are not real; they disappear when the full light shines on them.

Like the antelope being chased by the tiger, we often respond to danger in panic, thinking, *There is no time—I must do something!* Our hearts pound, we sweat, we gasp for air, we can think of nothing else: *I've got to get away!*

But stop a moment. Learn to respond properly to your times of danger. You don't need to "eat and run." Take time for a spiritual feast because the Lord has spread a table in the presence of your enemies, and your cup overflows.

Obviously, fasting from earthly food is not enough; we must also take time to eat heaven's nourishment. But after we have spent time with God, feeding on the bread of life, let's not be too hasty to jump up and start running again. Do we again start looking nervously around us for the *death shadow* that has been following us? Do we listen to the voice of the enemy that is trailing us as we go? No! The Shepherd has said, "Surely goodness and mercy will follow me all the days of my life." If we still think the *death shadow* is following us and we are still trying to get away, then we are looking for the wrong thing. When we fast, we learn to look to God. And when we see Him, we realize the sound behind us is not the enemy, but the sound of God following us: "Surely goodness and mercy will follow me." God will follow us all the days of our life. He will protect us and He will take us to live with Him in heaven when this life is over.

Have you ever walked through a dangerous situation, and your back tingled with fear? You didn't see the danger behind you, but you felt it was there because every nerve in your back itched. Maybe you feel they're going to fire you at work. Maybe you feel that your presentation won't be ready on time. Maybe you feel they will find something wrong with your report. You don't know why, but you feel a *death shadow* pursuing you at all times. You must learn to trust the Shepherd who says, "Surely goodness and mercy will follow me all the days of my life."

When you fast, tell yourself that it's okay to pause and breathe. God has invited you to a great feast of spiritual food: Do you know how to find His banquet? You fast from earthly food to find heavenly food. The meal is called *communion with God*, or getting to know God intimately through time spent with Him. Nothing else in life is worth knowing. When your desperation for God exceeds your fear, then nothing in life can scare you.

Now is the time to come to His table. The cups are full. The food is warm and ready. It's time to sit down and eat. The Lord is there, for He has said, "I will be with you." And what will you do after you finish eating? The promise is, "I will dwell in the house of the Lord forever."

Principles I Learned from Fear

- I am usually afraid of shadows that have no reality.

- I can walk through terrifying valleys if the Lord is with me.

- I need a shepherd because I am like a sheep that can't take care of itself.

- I have a spiritual banquet awaiting me when I go through life-threatening situations.

- I don't have to start running again after God feeds me at His table because goodness and mercy will follow me.

Journaling

It is hard to write about our fears because we're afraid someone will read about them and laugh at us. Also, we're afraid that writing our fears on paper will give them a large reality, larger than they really are. We think, *If I deny their size or ferocity, they can't hurt me.* In reality, the opposite is true. Writing out your fears is like turning on the light that dispels the shadows in your room at night. Writing answers to the following will help your journaling.

1. Write out the greatest fear that is stealing your happiness or confidence. Edit it to make sure the statement properly expresses your feelings.

2. As you walk through the Bible study, recognize and write what your reaction to your fears should be. Then, write how God is helping you deal with your reaction to your fears.

3. List your other minor concerns, then put them in order of importance. As you objectify your concerns, you may see some of them drop off your list.

4. Write a promise from Scripture, indicating how God would have you deal with the problem.

5. Usually fears fall into certain categories: fear of loss (e.g., loss of money, job, health, loved ones, intimacy); external fears (e.g., war, economic depression, plague); internal, personal fears (e.g., fear of heights, darkness, snakes, flying). What areas concern you?

Three-Step Bible Study

- Read the question.
- Read and analyze the Bible verse.
- Write out your response to the question.

1. God recognizes our fears. Notice how Jesus realized His disciples were afraid. What kind of things scared them? What kinds of things scare you?

"And when the disciples saw Him walking on the sea, they were troubled, saying, It is a ghost! And they cried out for fear. But immediately Jesus spoke to them, saying, be of good cheer! It is I; do not be afraid" (Matt. 14:26-27).

_____

_____

_____

_____

_____

_____

_____

_____

_____

2. Sometimes fears are justified. When is that? When have your fears been justified?

"For he [a civil ruler] is God's minister to you for good. But if you do evil, be afraid; for he does not bear the sword in vain; for he [civil ruler] is God's minister, an avenger to execute wrath on him who practices evil" (Rom. 13:4).

_____

_____

_____

_____

_____

_____

_____

_____

3. On what basis does God take away your fear? How can you claim this promise?

"My son, let them [wise biblical principles] not depart from your eyes—Keep sound wisdom and discretion; so they will be life to your soul and grace to your neck. Then walk safely in your way, and your foot will not stumble. When you lie down, you will not be afraid; yes, you will lie down and your sleep will be sweet" (Prov. 3:21-24).

_____

_____

_____

_____

_____

_____

_____

_____

4. When did the psalmist trust in God? What were the occasions you trusted in God?

"Whenever I am afraid, I will trust in You" (Ps. 56:3).

_____

_____

_____

_____

_____

_____

_____

_____

5. What should be your greatest fear?

   "And do not fear those who kill the body but cannot kill the soul. But rather fear Him who is able to destroy both soul and body in hell" (Matt. 10:28).

   _____

   _____

   _____

   _____

   _____

   _____

   _____

   _____

   _____

6. What is promised to those who fear God?

   "But to you who fear My name The Sun of Righteousness shall arise With healing in His wings; And you shall go out and grow fat like stall-fed calves" (Mal. 4:2).

   _____

   _____

   _____

   _____

   _____

   _____

   _____

   _____

Chapter Eight

Fasting to Listen to God

Hearing from God is one of the best things that can happen during a fast. When you take time to read the Word of God, pray, and wait on the Lord, you can hear the voice of God speaking to you. You stop listening to your body and catering to its desires so that your soul can become quiet. Then you can listen to God only.

Can you recall a time when someone was yelling to get your attention at a sports event but you didn't hear him? There were so many other voices—people yelling, music playing, your own cheering—that you couldn't hear your name being called. Often for the same reason we don't hear God speaking to us. We get so busy talking, working and yelling that we cannot hear Him.

There's another way we may miss the voice of God. Have you ever been so focused on what you were doing that you didn't hear your name being called? Perhaps you were watching a television program or were working at the computer. Someone called your name but you never knew it. It was not that you couldn't hear it, or that the voice was too soft or blocked out. It was a matter of inattention. You didn't hear someone call your name because you weren't paying attention.

Two things happen when you take time to fast. First, you slow down your system and become quieter so that you can hear God. Second, you take time away from your daily routine so that you can focus your attention on Him. Quiet and focus. Those are the results of fasting.

Listening can be difficult, but our failure to listen can cause consequences. For example, your automobile motor makes a strange knocking noise, but you don't notice it or just ignore it. Later, you pay the price of a new ring job. Or in a thousand ways your kids ask for your attention, but you're too busy. You pay the price of a rebellious teenager.

There are those who listen to the wrong voice, too. As Jesus and the disciples came to Caesarea Philippi, Jesus told Peter that He would build the Church on the Rock and that the gates of hell would not prevail against it. Peter heard (and listened to) that wonderful promise. When Jesus told the disciples He was going to Jerusalem to die, to be buried, and on the third day He would rise again, Peter heard Jesus. But he also listened to the deceptive inner voice of Satan. Scripture tells us, "Peter took Him [Jesus] aside and began to rebuke him, saying, 'Far be it from you, Lord'" (Matt. 16:22). Listening to the wrong voice got Peter into trouble. Jesus turned to Peter, "Get behind Me, Satan; you are an offense to Me" (v. 23). Judas listened to the wrong voice, too. Judas heard Jesus call him to discipleship: "Come to Me all you who labor and are heavy laden, and I will give you rest" (Matt. 11:28). But Judas listened to the inner voice of greed.

On the night before Jesus died, Jesus specifically warned Judas, saying, "He who eats bread with Me, has lifted up his heel against Me" (John 13:18). Surely, only Judas knew what Jesus meant. Or was he not listening to Jesus? Judas listened to the voice of money and lost his soul.

We can learn positive lessons about listening to God from Samuel, a young boy who heard God's voice even as a child. His mother, Hannah, had dedicated Samuel to Temple service. "Then the boy Samuel ministered to the Lord" (1 Sam. 3:1).

Samuel not only served in the tabernacle, he slept there so that he could be available if needed. Samuel had placed himself near enough to God to hear His voice when He called. "And it came to pass at that time . . . where the Ark of God was, and while Samuel was lying down, that the Lord called Samuel" (1 Sam. 3:2-3). Because Samuel was in the right place doing the right task with the right attitude, he was able to hear.

Samuel heard the voice of God in the middle of the night: "The Lord called Samuel: and he answered, 'Here I am'" (1 Sam. 3:4).

God may speak to you when you are driving the expressways, working, playing sports, or are as far removed from the church as possible. God may awaken you in the middle of the night. You cannot always predict when God will call. But you can always be ready to hear Him. You can assume the right attitude—an attitude of listening—and put yourself in a position where you are ready to hear Him when He speaks.

When God spoke to Samuel, the young boy didn't know who was speaking: "He [Samuel] ran to Eli [the priest in the Temple], and said, 'Here am I: for you called me'" (1 Sam. 3:5). Samuel thought Eli had called him. He hadn't recognized that the voice belonged to God.

Is it possible for us to fail to recognize the voice of God when He speaks? We have so many voices calling to us today, and we need to train ourselves to listen to God. A great pianist can hear "the song inside the song," but hearing at this deeper level doesn't come automatically. An aspiring pianist must give himself or herself to practice, to repetition, and to listening to other outstanding pianists. The pianist must do more than play the notes on the sheet music; he or she must commit to do whatever it takes to learn the new skill, and must desire mastery with all his or her heart.

And so must you. Hearing God speak to you is different than listening to the six o'clock news. Unlike the TV, God doesn't speak if the hearer isn't listening. You can hear God best when you are in a quiet setting with no distractions, no pressures, and no alternate voices.

John Maxwell taught himself to listen to people by taking a legal pad to important conversations. He wrote a large *L* in the upper corner of the pad. Every time he looked down and saw the *L*, he again focused on listening to what the other person was saying. When you are fasting, pray with a pen in hand and legal pad before you. Ask God to speak to you, and then write down what He says. You do this by writing down what you are thinking—what comes to your mind. Once you get it down on paper, you can come back to analyze the message to determine if it was from God or yourself.

We receive all types of thoughts when we are praying and fasting. Some are wonderful thoughts from God, and others may be conflicting thoughts from our recessive memory. Some thoughts come to us from our selfish nature to draw us away from God and point us in the wrong direction. When an inner voice is clear, purposeful, and does not bring confusion, it is probably from God. When it is disruptive, confusing, and points you in many directions, it is probably not from God.

And usually when God calls to you, He is persistent. God called young Samuel more than once: "The Lord called yet again, 'Samuel'" (1 Sam. 3:6).

What is our best response when we are listening for God's voice? Samuel was told by Eli, "Go, lie down; and it shall be, if He calls you, that you must say, 'Speak, Lord; for your servant hears'" (v. 9). When you think you've heard from God, continue to listen and hear again. Then it is best to yield to His will and do what He commands.

The Other Voice

I have found in my walk with God that when He speaks to me there is usually another voice pulling me in a different direction. Life has never been simple. We live in a world where we are tempted by the lust of the flesh, the lust of the eyes, and the pride of life. And because sin is so subtle, sometimes I'm not sure whether an inner voice is from God or from my own desires. So I try to picture life as a battle and realize that, in a war, when your Commander-in-Chief gives one set of directions, the enemy is likely to give you opposite messages. It is the same in football: When you hear the voice of the quarterback giving directions, there is an opposing lineman who wants to drive you into the turf. When Judas heard the wrong voice, he followed it to his destruction. So did Cain, Saul, and one of Paul's followers: "Demas has forsaken Me, having loved this present world" (2 Tim. 4:10).

Oh, that life was as simple as it used to be. It seemed easier to recognize God's voice. As children we sang, "I come to the garden alone, while the dew is still on the roses . . . and he walks with me, and he talks with me." But our lives have become so hectic. There are jobs, chores, demands, commuting, and traffic gridlock. We can't hear God because of confusion and frustration and anger and cursing. We need to come out of the everyday routine, slow down, get still, fast, and make time to listen to God.

How to Listen

There are some preparatory steps you can take as you seek to hear God's voice. Let these guide you as you seek His presence.

1. Get Ready

Think back to school and how you used to prepare for class. One of the best ways to fully hear and understand a teacher's lecture was to be ready when class began. This meant being in your seat with books open and pen ready to take notes. Getting your faculties and materials ready to listen helped you get more from a teacher's lecture. In the same way, when you fast and seek God, have your Bible open and your notebook ready, and tune your faculties to the voice of God.

2. Get Quiet

Often we can't hear the other person because we do too much talking. If we want to hear from God, we must quit talking so that God can speak. "Be still and know that I am God" (Ps. 46:10). If you do all the talking, all you'll learn is what you already know.

3. Get Focused

When you've got something important to say to a friend, you don't just blurt it out when you first see them. You get focused; you want them to pay attention to you. You wouldn't share something intimate with a person who wasn't listening to you, would you? God will not tell you an intimate thought, either, until He has your attention.

4. Get Rid of Distractions

When a man proposes to a woman, he doesn't want anything to distract them from the moment. He goes to a special place and makes sure he has her attention before asking the "BIG" question. You can listen to God anywhere—on a crowded commuter train, in your office cubicle, jogging or driving. A quiet place is best because there are no distractions, but such a spot is not always available. Learn to block out noises and distractions to listen to God. Watch the businessman reading the newspaper on the commuter train. He's not listening to the rumble of the train or to conversations around him. He is focused only on the newspaper. With a little effort, you can focus on prayer, reading or meditation.

5. Get Still

The concept of "being still" usually refers to the absence of physical movement, but not always. You can "be still" before God as you jog, exercise in a weight room, or fly on a crowded plane. The secret is developing a "still spirit"—

a listening spirit—and not just a still body. "Be still and know that I am God" (Ps. 46:10).

Principles I Learned About Listening to God

- I don't hear God because I am not listening properly.

- I must be in the right place with the right attitude to hear and understand God's voice.

- I will have difficulty hearing God because of the pressures of life.

- I can better hear God's voice when I am fasting.

- I usually hear a second voice when God speaks to me.

- I must be careful not to listen to the wrong voice because it can destroy me.

Journaling

When you fast to listen to God, make sure you don't do all the talking. If you have a question to ask God, write it in your journal (writing clarifies in your mind what you are requesting). Then write down all the answers that come to your mind. Later, sort through your notes to determine what is from God and what is not. Even if you have no anxieties or questions, still write down the impressions you get from God. Answering the following questions will help you hear and understand what God is saying to you.

1. What are the things in your life that keep you from hearing God?

2. What are the times and places in your past where you have best heard from God?

3. If you are fasting and praying about a problem or decision, write it down, and then ask God to help you understand the full nature and source of your problem. Keep editing the problem you have just written until it says exactly what you feel and want.

4. If you hear confusing directions, write down both messages, and then test them with Scriptures: "Test all things, then do what is right" (1 Thess. 5:21, author's translation).

5. If you feel you are not hearing from God, what must you do? Check your attitude by your list.

Three-Step Bible Study

- Read the question.
- Read and analyze the Bible verse.
- Write out your response to the question.

1. God originally created mankind to have fellowship with them. What was Adam and Eve's response when they heard the sound of the Lord? Describe your response to fellowship with God.

   "And they heard the sound of the Lord God walking in the garden in the cool of the day, and Adam and his wife hid

themselves from the presence of the Lord God among the trees of the garden" (Gen. 3:8).

_____

_____

_____

_____

_____

_____

_____

_____

_____

2. Normally, we don't hear the audible voice of God, but there was a generation that had that privilege. What did God's voice do for them?

"Did any people ever hear the voice of God speaking out of the midst of the fire, as you have heard, and live?" (Deut. 4:33).

_____

_____

_____

_____

_____

_____

_____

_____

_____

3. God speaks to you through many ways. What have you heard God say to you through nature?

"The heavens declare the glory of God; and the firmament shows His handiwork. Day unto day utters speech, and night unto night reveals knowledge" (Ps. 19:1-2).

_____

_____

_____

_____

_____

_____

_____

4. How does God speak to you through the Scriptures? Give one illustration from your experience.

"Only be strong and very courageous, that you may observe to do according to all the law which Moses My servant commanded you; do not turn from it to the right hand or to the left, that you may prosper wherever you go" (Josh. 1:7).

_____

_____

_____

_____

_____

_____

_____

_____

5. Who has God sent to help you understand His voice that speaks through the Scriptures? How can you better hear God's voice in Scripture?

"Now we have received, not the spirit of the world, but the Spirit who is from God, that we might know the things that have been freely given to us by God" (1 Cor. 2:12).

_____

_____

_____

_____

_____

_____

_____

6. What can you do to hear and understand God's Word? List the suggestions the psalmist gives to the one seeking to know God's Word.

"Blessed is the man who walks not in the counsel of the ungodly, nor stands in the path of sinners, nor sits in the seat of the scornful; but his delight is in the law of the Lord, and in His law he meditates day and night" (Ps. 1:1-2).

_____

_____

_____

_____

_____

Chapter Nine

Fasting to Open Up Heaven

Have you ever felt like heaven was shut to you? Sometimes you pray—you pray sincerely, you pray with tears—but your prayers seem to bounce off the ceiling. How do you feel when you can't get through to God in heaven?

When your prayers don't get through, add fasting to your prayers. Denying yourself earthly food demonstrates your sincerity to God. He can feel the integrity behind your words.

Leviticus 26 contains some wonderful promises of God concerning His response to His children. He promises that His glorious presence will dwell among His people: "I will set up my tabernacle among you" (v. 11). He promises to be near every believer: "I will walk among you and will be your God" (v. 12). He delivered Israel from Egypt and reminded them: "I have broken the bands of your yoke" (v. 13). Yet just a few verses later, after God had done everything for them, He warned them, "If you do not obey me . . . I will make your heavens like iron" (vv. 18-19). Is heaven iron to you? When God's people don't obey Him, He shuts heaven's door.

What Is an Open Heaven?

When we say there is a door to heaven, obviously we're not talking about a crack in the sky. Nor are we talking about a literal door into heaven. An "open heaven" is a figure of speech that means we have easy access into the presence of God. The Bible speaks of both a door to heaven (see Rev. 4:1) and a window to heaven (see Mal. 3:10). Both of these refer to access to the presence of God.

The murderous Saul had just supervised the death of Stephen. Now he was on his way to Damascus to arrest more Christians with the intent of putting them to death. Saul was a young rabbi, a rising leader in the party of Pharisees, and one who fanatically opposed Christianity, which he saw as a dangerous new cult. He was not seeking the presence of God, nor was he trying to find intimacy with God. Saul was not pursuing God as the young deer pursues the water brooks (see Ps. 42:1). No. Saul's passion was for eradicating Christianity.

While Saul was wrong, at least he was sincerely wrong. He sincerely thought he was carrying out the exact letter of God's Law. Like many legalists, Saul was committed to enforcing every "jot and tittle" of the Word of God, but he missed the God of the Word.

God stopped him in his tracks, knocked him off the horse to the ground, and blinded him. In that moment of revelation, Saul looked into heaven and saw Jesus. We might say he looked into heaven through an open door. God asked from heaven:

"Saul, Saul, why are you persecuting Me?"

"Who are You, Lord?" Saul asked.

"I am Jesus whom you are persecuting" (Acts 9:4-5).

In that encounter, Saul met Jesus Christ and was transformed. He became Paul, the apostle to the Gentiles, and the teacher of the grace of God to the world.

Paul was blinded by the encounter. His stubborn pride was humiliated. His servants had to lead him into the city to a house on the street called *Straight*. As a broken man, Paul fasted and prayed for three days, seeking the truth. The young rabbi who thought he saw all of the truth of the Old Testament was really blind to the truth. He had to come to the end of himself. Then the Lord spoke to him and showed him a better way.

Has Jesus ever come to you, knocking you off your horse to the ground, breaking your pride? Has the Lord ever opened your eyes to heaven? If He has ever come near, you will never forget it. We should long for those encounters and live for experiencing the presence of the Lord.

What's it going to take for you to open God's door? Jesus told us that the formula to open heaven's doors is to ASK. (The three letters of ASK form an acrostic of the command: Ask, Seek and Knock.) If you want to open heaven's door, you must, "*Ask*, and it will be given to you; *seek*, and you will find; *knock*, and it will be opened to you" (Matt. 7:7, italics added).

In the original language, these three verbs—ask, seek and knock—are in the linear tense, meaning continuous action. This indicates you should keep on asking, keep on seeking, and keep on knocking. Persistence is the way to open heaven's door, not just hardheaded persistence, but persistence with faith.

Have you ever tried to log on to your computer but your password wasn't working? That happened to me one day. I typed in my password and hit the *enter* key but nothing happened. I tried it again and again and again. Finally it worked. Persistence paid off. But my persistence was based on the faith—the absolute assurance that I was using the right password.

However, if I came to your computer and typed in my password, then hit the *enter* key, nothing would happen. No matter how many times I repeated the process, nothing would happen. My persistence would produce nothing but frustration. To open heaven's door, you must have persistence—but it must be educated persistence—knowing you're using the right password. What is the correct password? "Nor is there salvation in any other, for there is no other name under heaven given among men by which we must be saved" (Acts 4:12). Jesus is the password to heaven. Use His name to get what you want. "Whatever you ask in My name, that I will do" (John 14:13).

Persecution Opens the Door

When people are making fun of you or criticizing you behind your back, this is a time to turn your back on the oppression of the world and flee to God in fasting.

One of the early deacons and great preachers of the church was Stephen. The Jewish leaders of his day could not match his wisdom. Stephen preached the great sermon contained in Acts chapter seven, and what was the response of the Jewish leaders? "When they heard these things they were cut to the heart, and they gnashed at him with their teeth" (Acts 7:54). As they began to stone Stephen, God heard and responded. In the prelude to his death, God opened up the heavens to Stephen: "But he [Stephen] being full of the Holy Ghost, gazed into Heaven, and saw the glory of God and Jesus standing on the right hand of God, and said 'Look! I see the heavens opened and the Son of Man standing at the right hand of God!' " (vv. 55-56).

God has a special place in His heart for His children who are persecuted. Let's pray that none of us have to be persecuted for God to open up heaven to us. Rather, let's seek Him in love and faith. Then, because we pray, fast, and seek God's presence, He will open heaven and pour out a blessing on us.

Unified prayer will open up heaven also. Sometimes when heaven is *iron*, join with a friend to pray. Jesus promised, "If two of you agree on earth concerning anything that they ask, it shall be done for them by my Father in Heaven" (Matt. 18:19). Unity opens heaven to us like nothing else. When believers "agree together," they can go straight into the presence of God with their requests and get what they ask.

Ezekiel was God's servant who opened up heaven for a special task. At the beginning of his ministry, Ezekiel testified, "The Heavens were open, and I saw visions of God" (Ezek. 1:1). Ezekiel saw God, but he also saw the task God had for him to do. God was looking for a man to stand in the "gap"—someone to stand between heaven and earth, to receive the message of God and give it to sinful men. God told Ezekiel, "I sought for a man among them, who would make a wall, and stand in the gap before me" (Ezek. 22:30). When God opens up heaven for you, He opens it for a purpose. Ezekiel had to reach out with one hand to lost people while reaching out to God with the other hand.

If heaven is not open for your unsaved friends, will you be a "gap person"? This means you must reach out in faith and pry open heaven's door for them. When God opens heaven for you, then you must hold heaven open for others.

While writing this book, I was on the shuttle at the Atlanta International Airport. A man speaking a foreign language ran onto the car and then tried to hold the door open for his family. The shuttle door could not be held open even though the man dropped his packages and tried to hold them open with two hands. When the doors shut and the shuttle began moving, he yelled frantically to his family. I saw panic on his face. He was separated from his wife and children in a foreign country where no one spoke his language.

Do you have friends that need to enter the door to heaven? How frantically have you tried to hold open the door for them?

Jonathan Edwards brought revival to the American colonies twenty-five years before the American Revolution. Before preaching an important sermon, Edwards fasted and prayed for three days, going without food and water. He was prepared to preach a scorching sermon called *Sinners in the Hands of an Angry God* to his congregation in Northfield, Massachusetts. The sermon warned the congregation that they were like an insect in the hand of God being held out over the open mouth of hell, and that only the grace of God kept them from being dropped into hell.

As Edwards fasted (an absolute fast, i.e., no liquids) and prayed, something went wrong about two hours before the fast was over. He began to gag and choke for water. At about four o'clock Sunday afternoon, he was forced to drink water, and in doing so he violated the vow he had made concerning fasting. Edwards was a broken man because to him he had failed in his fast before God.

That evening a broken preacher stepped into the pulpit. Nevertheless, with a lantern in one hand and a fully written manuscript in the other, he read the sermon. The power of revival swept into the Northfield church and people reached out to grab the pillars of the church, feeling they were being swept into hell itself. God used the brokenness of Jonathan Edwards to begin what history calls The First Great Awakening. It was not his vow that God blessed; it was his brokenness that God worked through to bring revival. Jonathan Edwards became a "gap man" for the entire thirteen American colonies.

When you fast and pray, you can ask God to open the windows of heaven and pour out a blessing on others through you. You can bang on the gates of heaven so that God will convict the lost person of sin and bring him or her to Jesus Christ. Become a gap person who props open the door of heaven so that your friends and relatives might enter.

Jesus told Peter, "I will give unto thee the keys of the kingdom of Heaven" (Matt. 16:19). Peter was given the ability to open doors by the power of God. Perhaps Peter used the keys on Pentecost when he opened the gates of heaven to lost people by the preaching of the gospel. But it was not Peter the man that did it, but rather the power of God working through a spirit-filled man. All of those who follow Peter's example can open up the door to heaven by fasting, prayer, preaching the gospel, and standing in the gap for lost people.

Do you have any kingdom keys lying around? When you begin to fast, ask God to help you find some keys to open up heaven so that someone might get in.

Do you remember the sons of Korah from the Bible? There are twelve psalms attributed to the sons of Korah. While we're not sure of each son's exact name, we do know something about their family background. Korah rebelled against the leadership of Moses and the authority of God. When Moses sent for Korah to come to the tabernacle of God—where the presence of God resided—Korah refused to come. As punishment, Korah was swallowed up by an earthquake. Apparently this left such an indelible impression on Korah's sons that they had a fear of leaving the house of God. Their fear was coupled with reverence, and they had a lifelong desire to live within the house of God.

The sons of Korah are those who cried out, "blessed are those who dwell in your house" (Ps. 84:4). They were the ones who prayed, "My soul longs, yes, even faints for the courts of the Lord; My heart and my flesh cry out for the living God" (Ps. 84:2). The earthly ambition of the sons of Korah was stated in Psalm 84:10: "I had rather be a doorkeeper in the house of my God, than dwell in the tents of wickedness." They had experienced the presence of God in the tabernacle. Today in God's Word we can still hear the echoes of the sons of Korah praying, "Lord, just let me be doorkeeper in Your house."

Is that your prayer? As you fast and seek the presence of God, could you pray, "I would rather be a doorkeeper in the house of my God"? If that is true, keep the door open for yourself and others. A doorkeeper in God's house opens it for all to enter. This is accomplished by prayer and fasting—not by praying just for the unsaved, but by praying also for the growth of believers and for the victory of God's people over sin.

When you fast, you do not just stand in the presence of God to enjoy His intimacy. You pray for others, both saved and unsaved. Because you have found satisfaction in the presence of God, you want to share it with other people. You want to prop open the door so that others will enter and enjoy God with you.

Principles I Learned About Opening Heaven's Door

- Sometimes my prayers are not answered because heaven's door is closed.

- God wants me to open the door to heaven.

- I can open heaven's door by prayer, fasting and faith.

- I see Jesus through the open door into heaven.

- If I open heaven's door, I must keep it propped open for others.

Journaling

While you are fasting and praying, you will want to experience God's presence in heaven itself. Keep a record of your experience during your fast. Answering the following questions will help you keep a meaningful journal.

1. Describe some experience when you felt heaven was closed to you, that is, you felt God was not hearing your prayers.

2. How do you usually repent because of a "closed heaven" so that you can get through to God?

3. Describe some previous times when the door of heaven was opened to you.

4. What did you do to open the door to heaven?

5. Write a description of what happened or how God opened the door of heaven to you as you were fasting this time.

Three-Step Bible Study

- Read the question.
- Read and analyze the Bible verse.
- Write out your response to the question.

1. What prayers do not get answered? List a few times you felt God didn't answer your prayers.

   "If I regard iniquity in my heart, the Lord will not hear [me]" (Ps. 66:18).

   "Behold, the Lord's hand is not shortened, that it cannot save; nor His ear heavy, that it cannot hear. But your iniquities have separated you from your God; and your sins have hidden His face from you, so that He will not hear" (Isa. 59:1-2).

"Now we know that God does not hear sinners; but if any-one is a worshiper of God and does His will, He hears him" (John 9:31).

_____

_____

_____

_____

_____

_____

2. What has God promised to do with your prayers? List a few prayers God has answered for you.

"And whatever you ask in My name, that I will do, that the Father may be glorified in the Son. If you ask anything in My name, I will do it" (John 14:13-14).

_____

_____

_____

_____

_____

_____

3. How do you feel when God doesn't hear and answer your prayer?

"I will break the pride of your power; I will make your heavens like iron and your earth like bronze" (Lev. 26:19).

_____

_____

_____

_____

_____

_____

_____

4. List the four things you can do when God shuts up heaven to you.

"If My people who are called by My name will humble themselves, and pray and seek My face, and turn from their wicked ways, then I will hear from heaven, and will forgive their sin and heal their land" (2 Chron. 7:14).

_____

_____

_____

_____

_____

_____

_____

5. Scripture tells us that tithing is one thing you can do to open heaven. Describe what God did for you when He opened heaven.

"Bring all the tithes into the storehouse, that there may be food in My house, And prove Me now in this," Says the Lord

of hosts, "If I will not open for you the windows of heaven and pour out for you such blessing that there will not be room enough to receive it" (Mal. 3:10).

_____

_____

_____

_____

_____

_____

_____

6. Saul was a conscientious Jew, but he was wrong. God opened heaven to him and when he saw Jesus, he changed the direction of his life. What will fasting do to change your life?

"And he was three days without sight, and neither ate nor drank" (Acts 9:9).

_____

_____

_____

_____

_____

_____

_____

Chapter Ten

Fasting to Satisfy Your Hunger

Several years ago I looked out from the pulpit to see a mother coming down the aisle with a bundle in her arms, covered with a beautiful white cotton blanket. I knew it was a baby and didn't think much else about it. This mother had it all together. With a plastic diaper bag over one shoulder (the kind that has a section for the purse), she had come quietly down the aisle to find a seat. Her impeccable dress told me she didn't miss details. The baby didn't disturb the congregation during the announcements at all. But when I was about five minutes into my sermon, I heard a penetrating scream, "Whhhhaaaaaaa!"

The baby was either wet or hungry, and judging from the abrupt outcry, it was probably both.

Little babies are not concerned with religious formality—singing, announcements, or sermons. They don't care who is watching, who is listening, or who they disturb. The mother quickly rose, excused herself, and retreated up the aisle out into the foyer. The baby let out a yell all the way up the aisle. Babies know how to display their hunger and how to get what they want.

What about believers? Do we know how to announce our hunger to God? Do we know how to get God's attention? God said, "Open your mouth wide and I will fill it" (Ps. 81:10).

When we get hungry, we need to feed ourselves on God. We need to cry out until we are satisfied with spiritual food. "Oh taste and see that the Lord is good: blessed is the man who trusts in Him" (Ps. 34:8).

Let's look at the Temple in Jerusalem. Its atmosphere was kept reverent and quiet. Only the Levitical choirs praised God. But the religious atmosphere changed during the Passion Week when Jesus entered the Temple. The lame and blind were present, even though according to the Law those who were not physically whole were not allowed entrance. How they got there, we don't know. But hurting people know how to find Jesus. "Then the blind and the lame came to Him in the temple, and He healed them" (Matt. 21:14).

A few minutes later, another unusual thing happened: "the children [were] crying out in the Temple, saying, 'Hosanna, to the Son of David'" (v. 15). The Greek word for "crying" does not mean the sound of a children's choir singing in harmony. These children were loudly calling out to Jesus. The chief priests and scribes became indignant, expressing their criticism. However, the Master would have none of their hostility. He responded, "Yes, have you never read, 'Out of the mouths of babes and nursing infants you have perfected praise'?" (v. 16).

Is this the time for you, like a child, to announce your hunger? Do you need to cry out for God? Do you need to become like the little children in the Temple and the little baby in church, yelling out, "I don't care who hears me . . . I am hungry for God"? When are you going to say, "I don't care what anyone thinks of me. I've got to have the Lord"?

For hungry seekers, God has promised, "Trust in the Lord and do good; dwell in the land, and feed on His faithfulness" (Ps. 37:3).

Seeking God in Our Churches

Aren't you tired of going to church and going through the usual routines without getting fed from the presence of God? If singing is not enough, if preaching doesn't satisfy you, a fast from earthly foods may help you find the presence of God. God will meet you when you search out His presence, saying, "I'm not going to let you go until you touch me and change me."

Remember, God has made our intricate human bodies to run on fuel—food—and He has put within us appetites so that we are sure to store up enough fuel to keep our energy levels high. Just as God gives us an appetite for physical food, He has also put within us a spiritual appetite so that we become hungry—with a holy hunger—for God Himself. Did God not say, "Blessed are those who hunger and thirst for righteousness" (Matt. 5:6)?

There is a problem within our churches today. It seems our carefully planned worship services can get along fine without God's presence. This idea reminds me of the little boy in Sunday school who was asked to write a letter to God about what he learned in Sunday school. He wrote, "Dear God, we had a good time in Sunday school. Too bad you couldn't be there."

As I analyze the results of our church services, it appears that some have been functioning without God for a long time. How have we done it? We have practiced our music so that everyone likes the songs we sing. We have practiced our prayers, practiced our responsive reading, practiced our announcements—we've even practiced our sermons—so that people like them. We put the words to our music on the screen, along with Scriptures, photos, and video clips. We have done everything to attract and entertain people. It's just that we have lost the ability to attract the presence of God.

Now it's not wrong to attract people so that we can win them to Christ. But let's not hold out one hand to visitors without holding out the other hand to God. Let's hold out two outstretched hands—one to the lost and the other to God. Can we not do both at the same time?

When you come to church, what is your passion? Do you want to talk *about* God or *to* God? Do you want to learn about the things God did in the Bible times or do you want God to do something for you now? Do you seek a *blessing* from God or do you seek the *blesser* Himself? Do you come to worship because you are hungry? When your soul is empty, the only thing that will satisfy you is God Himself.

And what about God? What does God eat when He is hungry?

Remember the story of Jesus coming to Jacob's well in Sychar? It was a brutally hot day. The Bible describes Jesus as famished, sitting wearily on the edge of the well. The disciples had gone into town to buy "hamburgers" and apparently told Jesus that they would return shortly. But before they got back, a woman known only as "the woman at the well" approached the place where Jesus was sitting. She must have been uncomfortable with the presence of Jesus, knowing that Jewish men had nothing to do with Samaritan women. The woman had been married five times and was now living with a man but was not married to him. She understood rejection, having been divorced five times, so she probably expected more alienation from Jesus.

It was Jesus who broke the silence. "Give me some water to drink."

She asked, "How is it that thou being a Jew, ask a drink of me, which is a woman of Samaria?"

"If you knew the gift of God, and who it is who says to you, 'give me a drink,' you would have asked him, and he would have given you living water."

"Sir," she said to Him, "You have nothing to draw with, and the well is deep. Where then do You get that living water?" (paraphrased from John 4:7-11).

In spite of the woman's objections, Jesus penetrated her heart. He knew her heart was empty, and that only the Father could fill her longing. In spite of her objections, Jesus said, "Woman, believe Me, the hour is coming when you will neither on this mountain, nor in Jerusalem, worship the Father. . . . But the hour is coming, and now is, when the true worshipers will worship the Father in spirit and truth; for the Father is seeking such to worship Him. God is Spirit, and those who worship Him must worship in spirit and truth" (John 4:21,23-24).

The woman had come looking for cool well water, but ended up meeting Jesus Christ who offered her living water. "But the water that I shall give him will become in him a fountain of water springing up into everlasting life" (John 4:14). The woman was looking for inner peace and only God could satisfy her inner longing.

What was Jesus wanting from the woman? It wasn't physical water. Jesus had the eternal water of life to give her. But what did He expect in return? And what did the Father want from her? Did He need anything? God is all-powerful and has everything.

The only thing God wanted from her was worship. God feeds on, or finds satisfaction in, the worship of His people. When you fast and seek God's presence, you feed on God. But at the same time God enjoys your fellowship, and your worship satisfies Him.

When two people eat together, that is a form of fellowship. In Revelation 3:20, Jesus is pictured as knocking at our heart's door: "Behold, I stand at the door and knock. If anyone hears My voice, and opens the door, I will come in to him and will dine with him, and he with Me." When you invite Jesus into your heart, He will eat with you and have fellowship with you. As you worship Him, you are strengthened while He finds satisfaction in your worship.

My grandchildren do not talk perfectly—they talk "baby talk." Yet as a grandfather I love to listen to what they say—imperfect . . . rambling . . . disconnected . . . but transparent and honest. I love to talk to my grandchildren because I love them.

The same is true of the Father. He loves to talk with us. We are not as smart as the greatest theologian, nor are we as eloquent as the greatest orator, nor do we know everything as the greatest scholar, but we come to our Father in heaven like children, and He loves to listen to us and talk to us. When we become transparent and honest, God sits down and finds satisfaction in our worship and we find satisfaction in His presence.

If good sermons were going to save the world, people would already be saved. If good music was going to lift the people to heaven, they would already be there. If better-planned church services were what we need, we should be where we ought to be. But we're not there. What's missing? We need the presence of God in our church services and we need the presence of God in our quiet times.

When we become hungry, only God can satisfy us. When we become empty, only the presence of God can fill our earthly vessels. It ought to make sense to us, but many of us still don't get it. We bring our vessels to church—already full—and we wonder why God doesn't give us anything. Why? Because we are not empty. If God visited our life, where would we put Him?

A turkey dinner is a beautiful sight to a hungry man, but not to a man who is already full. We come to church full of sports, news, business and entertainment. We have no empty spot for God, so we can't receive what He gives to us. He cannot pour Himself into a full vessel, just as you cannot pour any more water into a full glass.

We must empty our vessels of "self" and the pursuit of selfish activities. And how do we empty ourselves? Several words come to mind: first, repent; second, yield; third, seek God; fourth, beg; fifth, pray in faith.

Can you imagine what would happen if you brought your empty vessel to God and in faith you asked, "Please fill me!"

The Bible says, "If you ask anything in My name, I will do it" (John 14:14). If we brought our empty vessels to God, we might hear in our hearts the sound of a mighty rushing wind. If we ask God to fill us, we might feel the cleansing flame of a tongue of fire. If we waited in His presence for His message, we might hear the tongues of God speaking to our ears.

It is when we desire and expect His presence that we receive a divine visitation.

Principles I Learned About Hungering for God

- I am usually afraid to let everyone know I am hungry for God.

- I develop a hunger for God by fasting.

- I don't find God in most church services.

- I can satisfy my hunger by worshiping God and at the same time satisfy His hunger.

- I must be empty for God to fill me.

Journaling

As you fast and hunger for God, keep a written record of your search for God. Write down what you think, feel and do. Answering the following questions will help you keep your journal.

1. List the various ways you feel when you are hungering for God.

2. What is the biggest barrier that keeps you from hungering after God?

3. How is fasting helping in your search to know God?

4. Describe an experience when you have had wonderful fellowship with God.

5. Read John 4:1-45 and list how you and the woman are similar. What did she do that you can do?

Three-Step Bible Study

· Read the question.
· Read and analyze the Bible verse.
· Write out your response to the question.

1. How did Daniel express his inner feelings? Write a description of when you were spiritually hungry. What did you do about it?

"In those days I, Daniel, was mourning three full weeks. I ate no pleasant food, no meat or wine came into my mouth, nor did I anoint myself at all, till three whole weeks were fulfilled" (Dan. 10:2-3).

_____

_____

_____

_____

_____

_____

2. Once, David fasted and prayed because of a sin he committed. How did he express his fast? Write out any experience you've had that is similar to David's.

"David therefore pleaded with God for the child, and David fasted and went in and lay all night on the ground. So the elders of his house arose and went to him, to raise him up from the ground. But he would not, nor did he eat food with them" (2 Sam. 12:16-17).

_____

_____

_____

_____

_____

3. Salvation is depicted as eating. How do you fulfill this picture in your life?

"And Jesus said to them, 'I am the bread of life. He who comes to Me shall never hunger, and he who believes in Me shall never thirst'" (John 6:35).

_____

_____

_____

_____

_____

_____

4. What good works must you do to be satisfied with bread from God?

" 'Do not labor for the food which perishes, but for the food which endures to everlasting life, which the Son of Man will give you, because God the Father has set His seal on Him.' Then they said to Him, 'What shall we do, that we may work the works of God?' Jesus answered and said to them, 'This is the work of God, that you believe in Him whom He sent' " (John 6:27-29).

_____

_____

_____

_____

_____

_____

5. God didn't tell you to completely stop eating, but to put a priority on all things. What priority should you put on earthly food and heavenly food?

"Therefore I say to you, do not worry about your life, what you will eat or what you will drink; nor about your body, what you will put on. Is not life more than food and the body more than clothing? Therefore do not worry, saying, 'What shall we eat?' or 'What shall we drink?' or 'What shall we wear?' But seek first the kingdom of God and His righteousness, and all these things shall be added to you" (Matt. 6:25,31,33).

_____

_____

_____

_____

_____

_____

6. When evil people persecute you, you should trust God and live a conscientious life in front of them. What does God promise if you do that?

"Do not fret because of evildoers, nor be envious of the workers of iniquity. For they shall soon be cut down like the grass, and wither as the green herb. Trust in the Lord, and do good; dwell in the land, and feed on His faithfulness" (Ps. 37:1-3).

_____

_____

_____

_____

_____

_____

_____

Chapter Eleven

Fasting to Worship God

Many times I wake up in a strange motel in a strange city and I don't feel like praying. When my airplane does not arrive on time and I get to the motel late, then I am not ready to wake up at six o'clock A.M. the next morning. When the telephone rings, my body aches. As I mentioned in an earlier chapter, I pray the Lord's Prayer before I get out of bed. I put my sweat suit on, get some coffee, and quickly read the newspaper. Then I return to my motel room to seek God.

I remember one particular morning when the angry clouds threatened rain. My tired bones creaked and it seemed like the walls of my drab motel were damp with humidity. I wasn't warm or cozy; I just wanted to go back to bed.

When I tried to pray, my words seemed to bounce off the ceiling. When I read the Bible, my mind drifted to other topics. I had difficulty keeping God in my thoughts.

But then something happened. I got on my knees, spread my hands to God in heaven, and began to worship Him, saying, "Thank You that I got some sleep. Thank You that I am physically able to get out of bed. Thank You that I am not sick. Thank You for an alert mind that can think."

I went on to tell God that I loved Him. The more I worshiped Him, the sharper my mind became. Within moments, the presence of God—the "atmospheric" presence of God—entered the room. I felt Him around me. The mildewed walls sparkled and the ceiling shined—not in reality, but in my soul. I felt the damp walls and cloudy skies no longer mattered. There was no sunlight to warm my day, but there was light from the Son to warm my heart. Suddenly, like the approach of a roaring train, I felt physical strength surge through my body, my mind was quickened, and I was ready for the day.

Entering God's Courts with Praise

We are all on a journey. From the time Adam and Eve were evicted from the garden, we've all been on a journey in search of God. And we all do it in various ways. Some search for Him in Buddhist temples; others in Islamic mosques. Some search for God on the Shinto's idol shelf; others in the Mormon Tabernacle in Salt Lake City. Perhaps the search is best pictured on the ceiling of the Sistine Chapel at St. Peter's in Rome, Italy. Michelangelo painted a man, representative of all of us, reaching out to touch the finger of God. Man is searching for God, hungering for God, longing for God. But not everyone finds Him because they don't reach in the right way.

When you look at the symbolic picture of man reaching for God, don't stop there. Look at God's face and look at God's hand. It is divinity reaching for humanity. Before you give up, remember, God is reaching out for you.

God visited the earth to dwell with the people of Israel in the wilderness. Moses built a tabernacle, and placed within its inner sanctuary (Holy of Holies) the Ark of the Covenant. It was to that ark that God came and resided among His people. Scripture says, "And there I will meet with you, and I will speak with you from above the mercy seat, from between the two cherubim which are on the ark of the testimony" (Exod. 25:22).

The tabernacle was a tent surrounded by a tall, seven-and-a-half-foot curtain wall that blocked the people's access to God. To approach God, the Israelites had to pass through the one gate into the tabernacle, bringing with them a blood sacrifice. God has always required a sacrifice to cover our sins when we approach Him, so worshipers brought a lamb, the rightful payment for sin. The death of the lamb was a substitute for the death of the worshiper. (Today we don't have to bring a lamb because, as John 1:29 states, Jesus is the believer's "Lamb of God who takes away the sin of the world.")

The psalmist describes the attitude that the people needed as they entered the gate to the tabernacle: "Enter into His gates with thanksgiving" (Ps. 100:4). Why is thanksgiving appropriate when entering His gates? First of all, to express thanks that there is a gate of salvation to God, where sins are forgiven. Second, to express gladness that God has permitted access to His courts to worship Him.

Inside the gate to the tabernacle, just outside the Holy of Holies, was the courtyard where the lamb was sacrificed. For the Israelites, drawing even closer to the presence of God—into His courts—called for praise. David sang, "And enter into His courts with praise" (Ps. 100:2).

Let us take a lesson from this today. The closer we draw to God, the more we will praise Him.

Inside the tabernacle, the Ark of the Covenant was located in the Holy of Holies. The ark was nothing but a large, gold-covered box (the word "ark" means box), similar in size to a cedar chest. The lid was solid gold and it was called the mercy seat. Just as a husband might sit upon the cedar chest at the foot of a bed to put on his shoes each morning, so God came to sit upon the mercy seat on the Ark of the Covenant. Worship was directed to the mercy seat, where God's glorified presence dwelt on earth. The psalmist describes God this way: "You are holy, Enthroned in the praises of Israel" (Ps. 22:3). In Israel, when the people directed their worship toward the Ark of the Covenant, God was present to receive it.

For us God is omnipresent, or present everywhere at the same time. We can worship Him anywhere. Just as He did for the Israelites, when I worship Him, He comes to receive my adoration. I can even bring God's manifest presence into a drab motel room by worshiping Him.

God is omniscient; He does not need any wisdom from us. God is omnipotent; He does not need us to do anything for Him. God is omnipresent; He doesn't need us to go anywhere for Him. There is only one thing that God wants from us and that is to worship Him: "The Father is seeking such to worship him" (John 4:23).

In the Old Testament God dwelt in the tabernacle. In the New Testament God dwells in our hearts. When Jesus met the woman at the well of Samaria, she reminded Jesus that her people worshiped on a particular mountain. Jesus reminded her that there was no longer a correct place to worship God. He told the woman, "The Father is seeking such as should worship him, and those who worship Him, must worship Him in spirit and truth" (John 4:23).

Today, so many people look for a *correct place* to worship God. But God simply wants us to approach Him with the *correct attitude*. We don't have to search out a church altar, nor do we have to journey to a lake at a Christian campground to find God. God is inviting us to worship Him at any time or place, as long as we do it in Spirit and in truth. We worship *in Spirit* when we give our whole heart in worship to God. We worship *in truth* when we come to God according to the Bible.

When Saul was rejected as king of Israel, what had been the criteria that God set for the man chosen to succeed him? God "sought for Himself a man after His own heart" (1 Sam. 13:14). God wanted a godly man to be king over His people. Samuel the prophet had gone to Bethlehem to name and anoint one of the sons of Jesse to be the next king of Israel (see 1 Sam. 16). Which one would it be? As each of the sons passed before old Samuel, he rejected them.

"Are there not more?" Samuel asked the father.

"Yes, there is one boy who is tending the sheep."

When young David passed before Samuel, he knew he was God's choice. And why did God anoint David king of Israel? Because in all circumstances David pursued communion with God and wanted to be near His presence to worship Him. David cried out, "The Lord is my light, and my salvation, whom shall I fear? The Lord is the strength of my life: of whom shall I be afraid?" (Ps. 27:1). Because he had a passion for the presence of God, he could say, "One thing have I desired of the Lord, that will I seek: that

I may dwell in the house of the Lord all the days of my life, to behold the beauty of the Lord, and to inquire in His Temple" (v. 4).

David was not a priest, so he could not bring animal sacrifices into the presence of God. The high priest had to bring animal sacrifices for David. But David understood the meaning of sacrifices, and he cried out, "Therefore will I offer sacrifices of joy in His tabernacle: I will sing, yes, I will sing praises to the Lord" (Ps. 27:6). What was the sacrifice that David brought to God? It was the sacrifice of worship. He magnified the Lord in the Temple. David said, "When You said, 'Seek My face,' my heart said to You, 'Your face, Lord, I will seek'" (v. 8). David understood that as he ran after God, he found God in worship.

Seeking God's Glory

God never let David build the beautiful Temple for worship on this earth. Although David had planned it, David's son Solomon built the Temple. And once it was constructed, God did not dwell in the house—immediately. Even when the Levites went into the house, God was not there—yet. Second Chronicles tells us, "Now Solomon assembled the elders of Israel, and all the heads of the tribes, the chief of the fathers of the children of Israel, in Jerusalem, that they might bring the Ark of the Covenant up from the City of David which is Zion" (5:2).

The ark was then carried upon the shoulders of the priests as demanded by the Lord: "The priests brought in the Ark of the Covenant of the Lord to its place, into the inner sanctuary of the Temple to the most holy place, under the wings of the cherubim" (5:7). After the ark was placed into the Holy of Holies, "It came to pass, when the priests were come out of the most holy place" then the entire congregation broke into great praise (5:11).

What happened when the people praised God? "Indeed it came to pass, when the trumpeters and singers were as one, to make one sound to be heard in praising and thanking the Lord, and when they lifted up their voice with the trumpet, and cymbals and instruments of music, and praised the Lord, saying, 'For He is good, for His mercy endures forever,' that the house, the house of the Lord, was filled with a cloud; so that the priests could not continue ministering because of the cloud, for the glory of the Lord filled the house of God" (2 Chron. 5:13-14).

God had come to dwell in His house on earth.

Some of us design a church service then ask God to come, but He doesn't. Some even fast for God to come but fasting doesn't guarantee God's presence. Like Solomon, we must prepare a place for God; it is then that God comes to dwell with us.

Some have had momentary encounters with God. Maybe God met you at the church altar one day or you had a "visit" with God at a special place. But how would you like God's "atmospheric presence" dwelling with you permanently so that you felt His presence every day? If you worship Him, He will come to you. If you build a place for Him, He will stay.

The passage in Second Chronicles goes on to depict the people's response to God's presence. "When Solomon had finished praying, fire came down from heaven and consumed the burnt offering and the sacrifices; and the glory of the Lord filled the Temple. And the priests could not enter the house of the Lord, because the glory of the Lord had filled the Lord's house. When all the children of Israel saw how the fire came down and the glory of the Lord on the Temple, they bowed their faces to the ground, and worshiped and praised the Lord, saying: 'For He is good, for His mercy endures forever'" (2 Chron. 7:1-3).

What is your response when God comes into your life? There should be a godly reverence. You worship God to get Him to come to you, and then worship Him because He is there. But don't forget godly fear. You cannot take the Lord lightly.

What do we mean by "godly fear"? This does not mean we are scared of God, or that we feel the fear a child will feel at a scary movie. When Isaiah saw the Lord, he cried out, "Woe is me!" (Isa. 6:5). Godly fear means "awe" and deep reverence. This also means conviction of sin. As we look at the history of the great revivals, men fell under the preaching of the Word of God. They fell with conviction as though dead, giving new meaning to the phrases "I was scared to death" and "I was so scared I couldn't move." We've known of people who have been paralyzed with fear so that they couldn't do anything when their car was screeching toward an accident. In this same sense, we fall on our face before God when we need His patience and forgiveness.

When God's Shekinah glory shines into your life, you will become like those in Solomon's Temple that day. You will fall on your face, bow in worship, to cry out, "The Lord is good, for His mercy endureth forever."

Some people know how to worship God with their head, but they never quite get it with their heart. They know the right answers and they can quote the right verses, but they do not "feel" God. God doesn't visit them. Yet, there are those people who desperately search for the presence of God and experience Him with passion in their life. Their heart pursues what others only know about in their head. They touch God and God touches them.

Ruined by Worship

There have been many days when I've had my devotions but God did not meet me. I've studied the Word of God but I didn't hear His voice. I've prayed all the way through my prayer list but not felt I really entered the heart of God.

And then one day, early in the morning, God met me in my devotions when I worshiped Him. I met with Him before the sun came up, not to get something from Him in answer to prayer, but simply to worship Him. Since I learned to worship the Lord, my morning devotions have never been the same. I couldn't go back to the old way. Touching God and having Him touch me had revived me. I could never again just read the Bible and pray. Remember Isaiah, who met the Lord and said, "I am undone" (Isa. 6:5). Just one encounter with God and you are unable to go back to playing church again. Your soul will rise to a new level of prayer and worship.

Use fasting to seek God more than any other time in life. No longer feed on earthly food but feed on the Lord. "I am the bread of life. He who comes to Me shall never hunger" (John 6:35). Heaven's food is so satisfying you will never be satisfied again living on just the food of this life. You will meet the Lord and He will change your life.

Principles I Learned Worshiping God

- I please God best when I worship Him.

- If I worship God, He will come to receive my adoration.

- I can feel the "atmospheric presence" of God when I worship Him.

- I must worship God in spirit; that is, with my whole heart, and in truth; that is, according to the Word of God.

- I can never go back to just daily devotion because in worship I touched God, and more importantly, He touched me.

Journaling

One of the most private experiences of mankind is one's worship of God. Therefore, it's difficult to describe the experience of worship in words. However, answering the following questions will help you write your worship experiences.

1. List some times when you read the Bible, prayed, and meditated on God, but God's Spirit didn't seem to be present. Why?

2. Of all the times God has manifested Himself to you, describe the most memorable experiences. What was your human response? What did God do for you? How did the experience change your life?

3. As you praise the Lord, make a list of the things and lessons for which you are most thankful. Keep this list for future times of praise.

4. Write out your prayers of worship to God.

5. Make a list of the many names of the Father, the Son, and the Holy Ghost. Praise God for the meaning of each name.

6. Take the praise psalms and pray them as a worship expression to God.

Three-Step Bible Study

- Read the question.
- Read and analyze the Bible verse.
- Write out your response to the question.

1. A foundational Scripture on worship is John 4:24. What is meant by the two conditions of worship, that is, in spirit and in truth?

   "God is Spirit, and those who worship Him must worship in spirit and truth" (John 4:24).

   _____

   _____

   _____

   _____

   _____

   _____

2. What are the different ways to worship God mentioned in this verse? How have you worshiped God in psalms? Hymns? Spiritual songs?

"Let the word of Christ dwell in you richly in all wisdom, teaching and admonishing one another in psalms and hymns and spiritual songs, singing with grace in your hearts to the Lord. And whatever you do in word or deed, do all in the name of the Lord Jesus, giving thanks to God the Father through Him" (Col. 3:16-17).

_____

_____

_____

_____

_____

_____

_____

_____

3. What is one of the basic reasons to worship God? How can you use this verse to worship God?

"You are worthy, O Lord, to receive glory and honor and power; for You created all things, and by Your will they exist and were created" (Rev. 4:11).

_____

_____

_____

_____

_____

_____
_____
_____
_____
_____

4. What is the foundational reason every believer should worship God? Stop to pray this verse before you answer.

"And they sang a new song, saying: You are worthy to take the scroll, and to open its seals; for You were slain, and have redeemed us to God by Your blood out of every tribe and tongue and people and nation" (Rev. 5:9).

_____
_____
_____
_____
_____
_____
_____
_____

5. In heaven you will worship God, singing the word "Hallelujah" (Hallelujah is Hebrew and Allelujah is Greek and they are the same word that means "praise the Lord"). What will be the motivation for worshiping God in heaven?

"I heard, as it were, the voice of a great multitude, as the sound of many waters and as the sound of mighty thunderings,

saying, "Alleluia! For the Lord God Omnipotent reigns"
(Rev. 19:6).

_____

_____

_____

_____

_____

_____

_____

_____

6. The last verse in Psalms directs our praise to God. Read the whole psalm and write the different ways you can worship the Lord.

"Let everything that has breath praise the Lord. Praise the Lord" (Ps. 150:6).

_____

_____

_____

_____

_____

_____

_____

_____

Bibliography

Anderson, Andy. *Fasting Changed My Life*. Nashville, TN: Baptist Book Stores, 1983.

Bright, Bill. *The Coming Revival: America's Call to Fast, Pray and Seek God's Face*. Orlando, FL: New Life Publications, 1995.

Bright, Bill. *Seven Basic Steps to Successful Fasting and Prayer*. Orlando, FL: New Life Publications, 1995.

Duewell, Wesley L. *Touch the World Through Prayer*. Grand Rapids, MI: Zondervan Publishing House, 1986.

Falwell, Jerry. *Fasting: What the Bible Teaches*. Wheaton, IL: Tyndale House Publishers, Inc., 1981.

Towns, Elmer L. *Fasting for Spiritual Breakthrough*. Ventura, CA: Regal Books, 1996.

Towns, Elmer L. and Jerry Falwell. *Fasting Can Change Your Life*. Ventura, CA: Regal Books, 1998.

Wallis, Arthur. *God's Chosen Fast*. Fort Washington, PA: Christian Literature Crusade, 1986.

Also Available in the Beginner's Guide Series

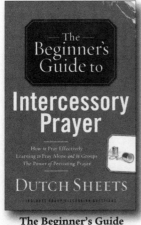

The Beginner's Guide to Intercessory Prayer
Dutch Sheets
ISBN 978.08307.45395

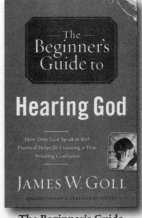

The Beginner's Guide to Hearing God
James W. Goll
ISBN 978.08307.46118

The Beginner's Guide to the Gift of Prophecy
Jack Deere
ISBN 978.08307.46026

The Beginner's Guide to Spiritual Warfare
Neil T. Anderson & Timothy Warner
ISBN 978.08307.46019

Available at Bookstores Everywhere!   www.regalbooks.com